The *Effective* Study Skills Handbook

We strongly recommend that students check with exam providers for up-to-date information regarding test content.

ISBN-13: 978-1927358702 (Complete Test Preparation Inc.)
ISBN-10: 1927358701

Version 8.5 March 2023

About Complete Test Preparation Inc.

Why Us?
The Complete Test Preparation Team has been publishing high quality study materials since 2005, with a catalog of over 145 titles, in English, French and Chinese, as well as ESL curriculum for all levels.

To keep up with the industry changes we update everything all the time!

And the best part?
With every purchase, you're helping people all over the world improve themselves and their education. So thank you in advance for supporting this mission with us! Together, we are truly making a difference in the lives of those often forgotten by the system.

Charities that we support -
https://www.test-preparation.ca/charities-and-non-profits/

You have definitely come to the right place.
If you want to spend your valuable study time where it will help you the most - we've got you covered today and tomorrow.

Published by
Complete Test Preparation Inc.
Victoria BC Canada

Visit us on the web at https://www.test-preparation.ca
Printed in the USA

Feedback

We welcome your feedback. Email us at feedback@test-preparation.ca with your comments and suggestions. We carefully review all suggestions and often incorporate reader suggestions into upcoming versions. As a Print on Demand Publisher, we update our products frequently.

CONTENTS

INTRODUCTION

OVERVIEW

WHAT IS THE SECRET TO SUCCESS AT SCHOOL? There is no concrete answer, but there are many proven techniques that help people succeed in school, whether it be high school, night school, College or University. First and foremost, maintaining a healthy balance between your social and school life is key. Remember that you are at school to learn and enhance your future. Meet people. Go out. Have fun. But don't forget your primary goal.

Studying.

There will be lots of it in store for you if you'd like to succeed in school. It is important that you have a plan for studying. Decide whether you will study in a group or by yourself. Think about how much time you have to devote to studying every day of the week and put study blocks in your schedule. We will go into detail and talk about how to do all this later in the book.

This next step seems like a no-brainer. Go to class. That's right, just go. Nobody will be looking after you to make sure you show up to school.

While you are at class, pay attention and take notes. Discover note-taking strategies that work best for you. We have a whole section on taking notes, because they are critical when it comes time to study for tests. Most students just 'take notes' and never think there may be different styles of taking notes. We present 5 different styles later in the book. Try them out and see how you like them and then choose one, or a combo, that works best for you.

Soon your study skills will be put to the first test - with your first round of exams. Don't panic. Use your study skills, develop a plan, and execute. Make sure you know when and where your exams are. Go to the room your exam will be held in. The last thing that you want is to be running around lost before an exam. After you finish your first round of exams, celebrate, and get ready to do it all over again.

School is a rewarding experience that you'll never forget. Make sure to spend your time during this part of your life wisely. At almost no other point in your life will your actions impact your future more than now.

MANAGING YOURSELF - GETTING ORGANIZED

TIME MANAGEMENT

The hardest lesson a student will ever need to learn is time management. Millions of dollars are spent on books, software programs, and equipment designed to help you manage your time. However, you are still likely to become overwhelmed with projects, assignments and the administration of your time management system. Time management styles are as complex and individual as the person. What works for one person will not necessarily work for another.

Often students have poor time management because they simply have no idea where to start with your assignments and day. A to-do list can help manage your workload on a day-by-day basis. Instead of being confronted with an entire textbook to read and feeling overwhelmed by the assignment, to-do lists break projects down into manageable sections that need to be completed each day. Large projects can be overwhelming, but once you start to break down the project and plan what you need to work on each day, you will soon begin to progress through your assignments and complete everything on time. Whenever possible, break big projects down into small manageable parts.

Later in this chapter you will learn about ways to use calendars and schedules to improve your time management.

PROCRASTINATION

Everyone studying is something that you have to deal with, but bad study habits can get you in trouble every time. That's probably because you are trying everything you can to avoid studying rather than just getting on with it!

Generally people actually spend more time and energy avoiding something than it would take to just do it!

Procrastination is the No. 1 bad habit of students who are supposed to be studying – but instead they make up every excuse they can think of to avoid it. Do any of these situations sound familiar?

- You are sick. You don't feel good. You think you are coming down with something. Usually it is just a delaying tactic, but sometimes your negativity will actually make you sick.

- You go to study with a friend and then end gossiping or going out to eat or for a drink and then the evening just gets away from you! Which is what you wanted anyway, and you let yourself just slide along!

- You are supposed to be studying with a study group but they arrive late, or, when they get there they are so disruptive no one gets any studying done.

- You turn on music and then end listening to that rather than studying.

- You go to sleep. This is the ultimate way to avoid anything. Just go to bed and close off the world hoping it will all go away!

- You say you are doing research on the Internet but just waste the time playing games and surfing.

- You HAVE to clean your room, make tea, have a shower ... anything first!

If you recognized these situations as all too common, you need to examine whether you even want to be taking the course or want to be in college or you just aren't interested in the subject at all. In other words – what motivates you? Do you want to be a nurse? A doctor? A lawyer? If so, and these subjects are part of the curriculum, then you need to re-evaluate your goals and make the decision that you want to be there and want the career you have chosen – or you need to go in a different direction.

Some people procrastinate because they are overwhelmed with the reality of dealing with a curriculum that is demanding and with some subjects that they are not interested in but are required and so they put off studying – hoping it will all go away – but unfortunately in life there is always going to be something that is distasteful or not to our liking and sometimes you just have to figure out how to get through it and move it.

So the best approach to procrastination is to examine it fully to decide what your real problem is. If you are just lazy, that is something else to be dealt with. However, if it is just a re-examination of your study habits, then you need to approach it in a positive fashion and break it down into manageable parts so that it is not so overwhelming. After a while it will get easier and easier, and you will have put it behind you!

Sometimes though, you just have to do things, and there is no way around it. Get used to it, get over it and settle down to deal with the situation as efficiently as possible and move on.

STUDENT TIP

Procrastinated by going onto online college admissions forums, comparing myself to everyone there, and then (surprise) feeling bad about myself.

Just don't. It's a) unproductive and outright self-destructive. It can demotivate you from doing well (i.e. "what's the point of trying if everyone else is so much better than me") and lead to you laying in bed and staring at the ceiling for hours pondering the purpose of it all (ahem).

If you procrastinate, procrastinate on things you enjoy. I took up dancing videos on YouTube during this time. It got me out of my chair, made me feel good about myself, and the good mood it created motivated me to study. Your breaks should be pleasant and rewarding (duh!).

If all else fails, take a nap. You're probably sleep-deprived anyway.

How to Handle Procrastination

Let's face it: for most people, studying is not fun. And most of us tend to put off things that aren't fun—especially studying. Honestly, this comes largely because of your primary school or even High School days. Back then, you could procrastinate a little—sometimes a lot—and still get decent grades. But then you get to college and BAM! your procrastination habit comes back to haunt you, because sloppy studying at this level won't get the job done.

Are you used to studying for that exam the night before, because that's how you did it in 12th grade? It's time to change those old habits.

There are many reasons you must not wait until the night before a test to start studying. First is the exhaustion factor. If you spend an all-nighter cramming for the exam, you're putting your body at its worst when it needs to be at its best. There will be a period during the night when you will become too tired to study and probably not finish going overall the information. And then when you crawl into the classroom, your brain will be arguing about whether it wants to take the test or go to sleep.

A Better Alternative

Break down the material you need to study into several smaller bites. Then study one or two small parts each day. Studying in this way will make the job a whole lot easier, and help you out on the exam. Each time that you successfully complete a smaller part, you reinforce your ability to complete tasks, making it that much easier to complete the next small part. Added bonus: You can feel all superior the night before the exam when all your friends are miserable studying for the exam and you're chilling in front of the TV.

Often there's just not enough time for you to cover all the material in one night. Here's a formula to remember: If you have more than three chapters to cover, you will not be able to complete it in one night. Two or three chapters is what you can realistically expect to master in one evening. So if there are, for instance, six chapters on the exam, allow three or four nights to study.

Another problem with procrastinating: What if something unexpected happens? Your computer breaks down and you can't get online to research, or you get sick and don't feel like studying one night. These and other crises are less of an issue if you have more time to deal with them instead of just one night.

Remember there's no test that you can afford to fail. You have to be on your best performance in every class in every unit. Part of making this happen is to successfully defeat the procrastination monster.

Getting Started & Being Realistic

Students often find it hard to settle down and get started or they study for too long once they do get started. If you find yourself avoiding settling down and getting started, or finding endless ways to avoid studying, then try to start studying for short periods of 10-15 minutes on a regular basis. When you find that you can sit and concentrate (which are skills that need to warmed up by this process as well) for longer periods, then change to a full study routine.

If you find that you study for too long, then it can seem much more of a chore than it really has to be. Even students who really enjoy their subject can end resenting the quantity of work they have to spend and start to avoid settling down to study.

A realistic study pattern (although it is better to find your own personal pattern) is that of a designated 2-hour session with a 5-minute break every half-hour. During the 5 minutes be mindful to get away from the studying and do something that is both relaxing and different (e.g. get a breath of fresh air). Make sure that you end the 2-hour session whether you have return to that point in the next 2-hour session.

Between sessions try to do something you enjoy or something new and refreshing. It is sometimes easy to view times of study as mundane, but they can also be times where you try new experiences and be creative. At first it may seem a little hard to think of things that you don't normally do and might enjoy and it is different for everyone.

Some examples may include going to the park, watching a DVD, painting a picture, going to a museum, meeting friends (but preferably not talking about study), learning a musical instrument, watching a sporting event that you do not normally attend, reading a novel, playing a new sport, etc...

It is important to attempt to change a revision period to a time where you are choosing to experience new things as well as choosing to learn new things, which is a more positive way to

approach studying.

TIPS FOR TIME MANAGEMENT

- Make a To Do List of all the things you are supposed to do everyday.

- Know what the best time for you to study is.

- Study the most difficult subjects first.

- Use of your spare time!

- Organize your Study area

- Don't be afraid to say no to if it affects your schedule.

- Combine activities as much as possible to save time.

- Schedule time for relaxation and entertainment.

- Try to get enough sleeping and eat properly.

- Review your notes daily

- Tell your friends what your schedule is to avoid distractions and conflicts. Don't waste time worrying about something you should be doing, just do it!

- Try not to be a perfectionist – usually it is a waste of time.

- Get a Wall Calendar and use it!

- Use daylight to study whenever possible. Studies show studying during the daylight hours is better.

- Keep a date book and write down all your assignment and the due dates.

- Take breaks. Several short 50 minutes sessions are better that one long session.

- Flash Cards are one of the most effective ways to study. Make Flash Cards and use them!

- Make Flash Cards or summary sheets and take them with you everywhere. Save time by using wait time to study. Study waiting for the bus, while you're waiting for class to start or for a friend to pick you up.

- If possible, schedule study time with a partner.*Choose your partner wisely however. Make sure you study, not socialize. If you schedule this just like you would soccer practice, or music lesson, it become routine.

STRESS MANAGEMENT

Students are under enormous pressure, and experience a great deal of stress. Keeping up with everything and making good grades is difficult in itself, but there are also the added pressures of work and relationships. When everything starts to seem overwhelming, the use of stress management techniques can make life easier.

Stress Management Tips

Not all stress management techniques are suitable for students because of the time involved. The following stress management techniques are not only are some of the most common, but also best suited to students:

- **Do not wait.** If you know that you have an assignment due, or an exam on the horizon, don't wait until the last minute to open your text. When you wait until the last minute, you increase your stress and anxiety, and your performance suffers.

- **Perform routine maintenance.** Just as a car needs maintenance, like an oil change, your body needs its own version of routine maintenance. You need to eat regular, healthy meals and get plenty of rest. In addition, take personal time to take a walk, go out with friends, or do other activities that you enjoy. Taking care of yourself will improve mood and performance.

- **Exercise.** Physical exercise not only is good for your body, but also relieves stress and works off negative emotions like anger or resentment. Engaging in physical activities increases your circulation, clears your mind, and boosts your overall energy level. Exercise also decreases levels of stress hormones, like cortisol, helping you to feel more relaxed.

- **Use relaxation techniques.** The use of relaxation techniques – like visualization, meditation, and breathing exercises – is a stress reliever that can be practiced any time. You do not need special equipment or a great deal of space for these, making them a great tool while sitting in the classroom preparing to start an exam.

Get organized. A major factor in stress for students is lack of organization. If you don't know everything you have to do, then it seems enormous and unmanageable. Once you know what you have to do, it somehow doesn't seem so huge. Make a schedule that shows where you have to be and when, as well as assignments that are due, and when exams are scheduled. Organize your study area so you can find books, notebooks, and pencils or pens quickly and easily. Simple organization will take care of missed deadlines and forgotten assignments, and it will prevent you from being stuck starting assignments at the last minute.

Basic Nutrition for Students

Studying and going to class everyday means you will be using your brain more than most people, and probably more than any other time in your life. You will need to keep your body health, and your brain nourished. Here are the basics that you need to follow to keep yourself healthy.

1) Practice old-fashioned eating habits. By that, we're talking about eating like they did 100 years ago. If possible, eat organic foods. Eat fresh vegetables, steamed potatoes, fruits, roasted chicken, and plain water. Here's the golden rule: If they were eating it a hundred years ago, it's probably better for you.

2) Some Organic foods are better than others.

Unfortunately the reality is food is an international commodity. Due to the heavy demand for some fruit and vegetables, chemical pesticides and fertilizers (which are bad for your brain) are use more heavily on some foods than others. Here is a full list of 'must buy organic' foods.

3) Include protein in every meal. This is important because it helps get your metabolism going. And that makes it more likely you'll lose fat, or you won't put it on in the first place.

4) Make a commitment today to swear off all carbonated beverages. They contain too much sugar--most of which will convert to fat in your system. And don't make the mistake of thinking a diet soda is much better; it's not. Those artificial sweeteners, while lacking the calories, have most of the same negative effects of regular cane sugar.

5) Add some healthy fat to mealtime. Yes, there really is such a thing! We're talking about polyunsaturated fatty acids, which are found in fish, seafood and vegetable oils. Especially good is virgin olive oil, so use it as a salad dressing or even in protein shakes. Healthy fats help burn bad body fat and build muscle-building testosterone.

6) Don't think that working out cancels out all the junk food you eat. It doesn't. In fact, nutritionists now say that proper nutrition is the more important of the two legs of fitness. The less your body wastes time cleaning from the junk you've fed it, the more time it has to build itself. It's that simple.

7) Water yourself. We mentioned this in number 1, but drinking the right amount of water is key to proper fitness. Water does a few things. It helps you feel fuller so you're less likely to overeat. It helps clean your system. It also helps with proper body metabolism. And finally and most importantly, it keeps your body hydrated without the need to resort to those more tempting sodas. Think of it this way: If you drink a glass of water when you recognize you're thirsty, you'll be less inclined to want a Coke or Pepsi.

These six essential steps, more than anything else you do, will keep your body and brain healthy and nourished.

Super Foods for Studying

Day One Of Seven:

Start out studying by creating an outline for the class you'll be taking an exam in. Break down your curriculum into units, chapters and main points. Under main points, write out definitions of new words and explain key vocab. These will be made into traditional flashcards or digital flashcards and studied on this day until they are thoroughly memorized.

To retain the memory of all these flashcards you've made, eat some fatty fish such as salmon, tuna or sardines (either canned, broiled, baked or boiled) for lunch on this day. Studies show that fatty fish is a rich source of omega-3s, helping long-term memory and improving mood. Perfect for the first day of memorizing lots of terms.

Day Two Of Seven:

Reserve this day for reading and testing yourself on the exam. Read over the main points of each chapter and predict what questions your professor/teacher may ask you on test day. Write these questions down in a Word document, Quizlet, or any other studying site to help you simulate what exam day may feel like. Sometimes, a textbook will provide end of chapter questions. This is a great tool for predicting what teachers may put out on tests, because most of the time, they will either put these exact questions or variations of it on the assessment you'll be taking.

To improve cognition in this stage of studying, snack on some nuts during studying. A 2014 review revealed that nuts such as walnuts, pecans, and almonds, can improve cognition and understanding. Furthermore, a large study found that female who ate nuts regularly over several years were found to have sharper memory than those who did not eat nuts. The nutrients in nuts like vitamin E and healthy fats, may clarify why nuts are so beneficial to the brain.

Day Three Of Seven:

Grab all those notes and materials of yours you have lying around in your folders. Organize these by chapters, and study these from top to bottom. Highlight points that you don't understand or cannot seem to memorize. Write all these highlighted points down for tomorrow's session and then follow this tip for memorizing it, read it aloud two times, write it three times, read it four times (this is called the two, three, four method). Repeat these steps until these points are memorized and understood. Teachers and professors do not give out pointless notes, and usually give notes that are useful on test day. Believe it or not, most professors want you to pass their class. How to study textbooks

To improve memorization skills for this day, eat blueberries for breakfast (In a smoothie, into some cereal, added into oatmeal, or even just eaten alone). A study done in animals showed that incorporating blueberries into their regular diet improved memory and delayed short-term memory loss. Great for a delicious breakfast and for a memory that will remember every point in your notes.

Day Four Of Seven:

Today is the day you and your professor will switch places. Take the notes from day three and teach them until you can do it without the notes. It doesn't matter who you teach it to, a family member, a pet, or even a pillow! Just make sure to teach it thoroughly enough until you can do it without notes and without your audience becoming confused. By teaching the content you'll need to know for your exam is the best way to know what mistakes you may make on test day. These can be clearly caught by you when you are unsure of a topic you are teaching or fail to mention a crucial point to your audience.

To teach clearly, one needs to clear their head of brain fog. The best food to do that are pumpkin seeds, which are high in iron. Those who have low iron levels often have brain fog and decreased brain function. Incorporate these pumpkin seeds to your diet by adding them to a sandwich for a pleasant crunch or sprinkling them onto a salad for some savory flavor.

Day Five Of Seven:

Time to power through those questions and flashcards you made on day one and day two. You should repeatedly answer these questions until you are thoroughly familiar with them and can answer every one of them correctly. Skim through your organized notes. Are there any highlighted terms you still can't understand? Then search up questions on the internet dealing with the subject an answer those until you are familiar with them. Create another thorough mock test with these questions. Include essay and multiple-choice questions with this simulation test. In addition, create an answer key. Do not use this study test for today. To avoid feeling sluggish on this day, drink coffee. Coffee is composed of two main components, caffeine and antioxidants. These can increase mood, alertness and concentration, helping you power through your fifth day of studying. Don't let yourself get lazy yet!

Day Six Of Seven:

Use the test you made of day five to simulate what exam day might feel like. Find a quiet room, start a timer and start the test. When you have completed the test, check your answers by looking at the answer key you've made. Retake this test as many times as you like until you are comfortable with the material. Any subject you feel shaky on should be reviewed with flashcards and the two, three, four memorization method. Practice Questions

In order to ace this mock exam, you need to be focused and anxiety-free. Green tea is perfect for this as it contains components such as L-theanine that help reduce anxiety. In addition, a study done with green tea has found that it helped improve performance and focus. Green tea would also help you become alert in the morning because of the small amount of caffeine it has.

Day Seven Of Seven:

Use this day to relax and not worry about this test. This day is meant for reducing anxiety before test day in order to do your best on the test. If you feel the need to study, quickly skim over your organized notes and flashcards, otherwise, refrain from heavy studying like you've done for the past few days. Remember to get an adequate amount of sleep on the day before your exam. Sleep will help you wake up fresh and alert in the morning.

The food to eat on this day is oatmeal—not for breakfast, but for dinner instead. Oatmeal naturally raises your blood sugar, which in turn, makes you feel sleepy. Oatmeal also contains melatonin, a natural hormone that helps you sleep. This food is perfect before test day to get good sleep and ace that test!

Test Day:

Eat some broccoli for breakfast today. Broccoli contains high amounts of vitamin K, which is linked to having a better memory. Before going into the test, snack on some dark chocolate. Chocolate has been found to be a mood booster. One study found that participants eating chocolate experienced higher amounts of positive feelings. What to do in the Test Room

Remember that you've studied hard for the past week, your hard work will pay off!

ADDITIONAL TIPS:

Keep distractions away from you while studying. Refrain from going to social media websites and lock away your cell phone in a cupboard or give it to a parent. If you are studying online, use www.coldtrukey.com, a site that blocks certain sites for an allotted amount of time.

Another tip is to create a quiet place for your studying. Use your room, a basement or go to your public library to have a place that you can concentrate in. Creating a productive study space

Always divide studying into sessions. Create thirty-minute sessions, with fifteen-minute breaks in between. Creating studying sessions longer than this can make it harder to recall memories, as you are cramming in more information you can handle at a time.

Learn to relax before you take your exam. Do not drink coffee or tea before your exam to wake up, high amounts of caffeine before a test (not a studying session) can increase heart rate, heightening anxiety during the test. When answering test questions, do not linger too much on a question you cannot answer, and come back to it on at the end of the test. Sometimes, you my find the answer in another test question, or looking at it with fresh eyes may help you recall some memory from studying to help you answer the question correctly.

BASIC EXERCISE FOR STUDENTS

Whether you are working hard, studying hard, or playing hard, you have to keep your body in top physical shape or sooner or later you will crash. Physical exercise is especially important when studying, since you are using your brain more than normal. Physical exercise increases the blood flow to the brain, delivering oxygen and nutrients needed to build new brain cells.

Physical activities tend to get lumped into the broad category of "exercise." There's exercise designed to help you lose weight, to help you build muscle, and even to help you fight off disease. Weight-loss activities might include walking, swimming, running, cycling, skiing, or even aerobic dancing. Muscle-building activities could include anything from push-ups to weight-lifting. Even though these exercises help you in different ways, all of them cause you to perspire, to breathe heavily, and to raise your pulse. Each of them also helps improve your health.

But what are some common suggestions that will help you get the most out of your exercise regiment? Here are some top suggestions for success in your workouts:

1) First, get started right. This means if you haven't exercised for a long time, are obese, or have a high risk of heart disease, talk your doctor before you start exercising regularly. Also, select activities which you enjoy and which do not overly-tire you. And then switch it up from time to time to keep things fresh.

2) Wear the right clothes. This means that your shirt and shorts or sweats should be loose fitting and appropriate for the activity and the weather. As for shoes, make sure they are comfortable and fit correctly.

3) Make it convenient. By this, we mean select a time that fits in with your schedule. Also find a place that is convenient to you. Place and time are important, because you don't want to give yourself an excuse for not doing your workout. Convenience makes it more likely that you'll turn exercise into a habit.

4) Entertain yourself. You'll be more likely to keep your exercise appointment if you incorporate something such as music. Or perhaps exercise in a room where there's a TV that you can watch as you work out.

5) Create a support network. Many people don't like to tell people that they've begun an exercise program. However, you should. Tell a few trusted friends and ask them to check to keep you motivated.

6) Remember to exercise the whole body. You might find it easy to exercise the biceps, but find leg exercises difficult. All the more reason to concentrate more on the legs!

These six tips, if you concentrate religiously on them, will help you create a better body--a better you.

A Good Night's Sleep

Sleep is a very important component to good study skills. Studying requires that you are fully awake and alert. Concentration and studying is hard work. Teenagers should be getting between 8-9.25 hours of sleep a night to be fully functional the next morning and have successful recall of their studying from the prior night. Adults should get at least 7.9 hours a night. (for more information see the National Sleep Foundation website) Less than 6 hours of sleep has been proven to be detrimental, so make sure you are actually sleeping and not cramming non-stop.

If you do have to go without sufficient sleep, be sure to catch up on it later. It may seem as though you are getting away with it, but it will catch up with you eventually. The "sleep deficit" that builds up over time and will affect your performance. If you think you may be suffering from sleep deficit now, try this test:

Poor sleep can make you inattentive and slow, forcing more all-nighters, increasing the sleep deficit. It's a bad cycle, and one you can avoid by staying on top of things.

CAFFEINE - GOOD OR BAD?

When you're on deadline with a paper to write or some serious remedial cramming, the first thought is to turn to caffeine to stay awake. For some people, it helps. But is it a good idea?

How it works: Caffeine is a stimulant. It makes your blood pump faster and keeps you from feeling sleepy so you can get the job done. This is why people have it first thing in the morning.

Where is it? Caffeine is everywhere. It is in colas and coffee and tea, obviously. It is in chocolate. You can also find it in drinks like Red Bull. However, it also lurks in places you wouldn't think — some brands of root beer and orange soda, Mountain Dew and, ironically, in Mellow Yellow.

Energy drinks have further complications, because some contain ephedrine as well as caffeine. You can read more about the complications here:

Caffeine helps in the short run. It gives you a jolt, so you can stay awake to follow what the professor says or to finish up a paper. However, you don't know when it will wear off, so you might not be able to get to sleep once the paper is done. And when it does wear off, you will feel as low as you did high when it first kicked in.

How much is safe? For children, Health Canada recommends no more than one caffeinated beverage per day. Pregnant women should have no more than two, and everyone else should limit themselves to three.

In the long run, it's better to keep yourself from needing caffeine. However, if you need it, a little won't hurt and can give you the jolt it takes to get the job done.

GETTING MOTIVATED AND STAYING MOTIVATED

Where do you look for motivation? To your parents? Your friends? Within yourself? Have you written down your goals for the current term? For your college experience? For your future?

Some people are intrinsically motivated. They are high achievers because they are driven from within to do well. Some people need extrinsic motivation, that is, an incentive or a reward – or even fear of a punishment. Knowing which group you fit into will help you figure out how to set the appropriate goals and motivate yourself to achieve them.

If you are driven to earn an A in every class and are already thinking about applying to the best graduate schools, chances are you have all the motivation you need. If your parents will stop paying for school if your grades fall below a certain level, that's a pretty good motivation, too.

But most people need to figure out what is realistically attainable, then plan out a course of action to get there – and reward themselves when they do.

ACADEMIC GOAL SETTING

Successful people don't just float through life; they set goals and live life intentionally trying to reach those goals. This is true of college students, as well. To truly reach your potential during your higher education, you might set challenging goals. What follows is a goal-setting strategy.

Any goal-setting strategy must include the following steps:

1) You must first know what you want to achieve in your studies. Ultimately this might be to get a career in your chosen area--which means your studies will focus on learning that career field. Some shorter-term goals could include raising your grade in biology or getting a 3.5 GPA.

2) From these goals, you then develop an action plan. The action plan is something set down on paper that you follow everyday to meet your larger goals. For instance, if your goal was

3) Measure your progress frequently to see how far you've progressed and what you still need to do to reach your goals.

4) After you reach each small goal, reward yourself. For instance, you could treat yourself to pizza or movie after reaching a small goal. The reward could be bigger for more major goals.

5) Make sure you follow your action plan, taking steps to reach your goal everyday. It's a basic law: If you move towards a goal a little bit at a time, you will eventually reach it, as long as you never stop.

Well-Defined Goals

When you write down your goals, as in step 1, it's important that they be well-defined. You know a goal is well defined when you can either specify the outcome as actions or you can measure the outcome numerically. For example, a poor goal is, "I want to do well in my economics class." This is not in any way measurable. However, saying "I want to make an "A" on at least 3 of 5 exams" is a better goal because you can measure its success. Likewise, saying "I will work one hour a day for the next month on my history paper" is a good goal because you have specified your outcome as an action.

Areas Where You Should Get Goals

- Doing well in your studies will require that you set goals in multiple areas. These five are the most important:

- Goals that help you allocate the right amount of time to important activities, such as studying and homework

- Goals that help you listen effectively in your classes

- Goals that help you understand your textbook

- Goals that help you improve skills in taking notes

- Goals that help you with test preparation and test results

- Goals that help you develop a better memory.

GOAL-SETTING QUESTIONS

The key step to setting the right goals for yourself are to ask yourself key questions. The answers to these questions will let you know what goals to set. For example, ask yourself:

What are my career goals, and what classes help me achieve them?

What skills and knowledge will I need to get into my chosen career?

What aspects of this course will help me acquire the training I need for my chosen career?

Which course will provide the biggest obstacle to me getting a high grade-point average? What should I do to make sure that I do well in this course?

Which class will require the most out-of-class study time?

What materials from this chapter am I likely to need to know to do well on the coming exam?

Was my last exam grade satisfactory? If not, what went wrong? What must I do to fix it?

Once you have the answers to these questions--and others that you think are appropriate--you will be in a better position to put your new goals on paper. And remember: No goal is carved in stone. Feel free to adjust them as needed.

Your Academic Goals Notebook

Earlier, we discussed the idea of setting goals while you're in college, but did so more on a theoretical level. Now let's get down to the nitty-gritty and talk about how to put some concrete goals down on paper and do move toward completing them. The best way of doing this is by developing a goals notebook.

Your goals notebook should have lots of paper in it and at least two dividers to separate three different sections. At the back is a section entitled "Long Term Goals." The front section is a section entitled "This Week's Priorities." And smack dab in the middle is the "Short Term Goals" section--which covers things that don't need to be done this week, but do need to be done something in the next few weeks or months.

Setting Long-Range Goals

While it's certainly a good idea to have long-range goals set for the rest of your life, our goals notebook will pertain specifically to your college goals. So for our purposes, long-range goals refers to what you hope to accomplish between now and graduation time. Filling in this section starts with a brainstorming session. Title one page, My Goals for My College Career. Make sure you're in a place where you will not be distracted and relax and think. Think about everything you hope to finish between today and the day you graduate. Include anything, whether it's school-related or not: Get an A in Economics, get a 3.6 GPA, go to Miami for spring break, get a fish aquarium, go skydiving once, get engaged. Try to fill up your page with at least 50 goals. At this point, don't get bogged down with thoughts of whether you can afford this or other obstacles. Just concentrate on things that you would like to do.

Once you've completed your list, read through them. You should be able to sense within yourself as you read something whether a sense of excitement jumps up in you, telling you that this is really an important goal to you. If anything does not bring that feeling of excitement, cross it off your list--UNLESS it's an academic goal. Usually the academic goals will not excite you, so leave all these on your list.

Hopefully you're left with only about 15 or 20 goals now. If not, go back and see if there are any more items you can cross off until you're left with just the cream of the crop goals. Now take each goal and, on another page, write down a date when you think you can realistically achieve that goal as well as 4 or 5 steps, in order, that must be taken to achieve that goal. We'll come back to these steps when we come to the This Week's Priorities section.

Setting Short Term Goals

In the short-term goals section, we're concerned primarily with your classes. This is the section where you will put items such as complete term paper for biology class or meet with my lab partners, and other class-related items that don't have to be done this week. This is a very simple part of the notebook. It can be just a few pieces of paper with simple statements of what needs to be done, along with a date for when it needs to be done or completed.

This Week's Priorities

This section entitled This Week's Priorities is where you really begin tackling all your goals, both immediate, short-term and long-term. Because your academic week probably starts on Monday, you will want to set aside some time every Sunday evening to update this.

Keep in mind that the biggest problem that disorganized people have is focusing on the urgent rather than the important. For instance, if you have an exam tomorrow in a one-credit class, you will be tempted to over-focus on it rather than continuing to study for a three-credit class that also meets tomorrow, but does not have an exam. In reality, because the three-credit class affects your grade point average more, it's more important to continue studying for that class, but most people will neglect that more-important class for the more-urgent one. A properly-done goals notebook helps to fight that tendency.

You should start a new page entitled This Week's Priorities for each week. At the top, put down the date that the week starts and ends, for instance, February 3 - 9, starting on Monday and ending Sunday. Now create 6 categories and space them out evenly from the top of the page to the bottom: Exams, Other Class work, Extracurricular, Chores, Relationships, Personal.

Next, it's time for another brainstorming session. Think of your next 7 days: In an ideal situation, if it were possible, what do you think you think you should accomplish this week? Write everything down on a scrap piece of paper. Now go through that list and if you have more than 20 or 25 items, eliminate the things that can perhaps wait until next week until you get down to no more than 20 or 25 items (That will average 3 or 4 that you're able to do per day).

Now take each of the items that remains and place them in one of the six categories. If you have an economics class in 2 weeks, it should go in the Exams section, since you want to study early. If your history paper is due in three weeks, put it there so you'll be reminded to start on it. Laundry can go in chores, a trip to the gym will go under personal, and calling home goes under Relationships. By dividing these items into categories like this, you immediately make that paper due in three weeks as important as this Tuesday's economics exam. In other words, it keeps you focused on the important, not just the urgent.

Now let's go back to our Long-term goals. Check out the first steps you put down for each of these. Every week, you should pick two or three of these steps toward your long-term goals to also complete during the next seven days. So pick two or three of these goals and place them in one of the six categories.

Now on you're on your way. Your goals notebook will keep you on track, not just this week, but throughout the semesters to come, and help you to eventually reach all your goals.

Managing your Environment

Productive Study Environments

To understand and retain information, you need to be able to concentrate on what you are studying and to concentrate you need a study spot that is comfortable and free of distraction.

Here are some tips and tricks to help you create a productive study space:

Identify your needs. Some people need absolute quiet when they are studying, while others prefer to have music playing in the background. You know what you need to help you concentrate and stay focused, so set up your study area accordingly.

Set up a study place that is equipped for studying. Pens, pencils, paper, calculator, pencil sharpener and other supplies should be within easy access of your study area. If you need to get up and move elsewhere every time you need something, you will not be able to stay focused on studying.

Be consistent. Use the same study area every day, and try to study at the same time each day. This establishes a connection between the time and space and studying, and going to your study space at the same time every day will become habit. Use your study area only for studying and you will associate that place with studying. That will help you stay focused on your studies while you are there. Make sure your study area is a place where you can relax, yet stay focused. Your bedroom may seem like a great place to study, but you may doze off continuously while studying there

Set up study rules. If you study better at certain times or when you are able to take short breaks, then make that part of your study rules. Make sure others realize that's part of your study routine.

Use study totems. Athletes have lucky socks or lucky shorts. You can have a study hat or study scarf. You can use a figurine, a toy, or any other type of object as your study totem. When it time to study, put on your study item or set out your study totem. A study item or study totem helps you study in two ways:

> Once others understand what your study item or totem means, seeing it will tell them you are studying so they will not interrupt you.

> When you start having trouble concentrating, you can look at your study item or totem instead of staring into space. It helps refocus your mind on the task at hand.

Your study area should be comfortable. The temperature should not be too hot or too cold. Make sure your chair is comfortable and you have room to wiggle your toes. Being confined or uncomfortable will become a distraction during a study session.

Establishing good study habits begins with setting up a productive study space. Your space should meet your needs, and personalizing it is always a good option. When you have a space used only for studying, it is easier for you to concentrate on the materials and ignore or avoid distractions.

TIPS FOR ORGANIZING OUR STUDY AREA

Centralize everything important to your daily life, either on a bulletin board, wall space, or on the back of a door. This area will be considered the area which you put everything important to you, such pictures, tickets to the concert and so on. With a centralized area, you are able to find everything you need without searching the whole house.

Get a Wall Calendar with large squares for each day. A wall calendar is extremely important for helping you keep track of your schedule. Everything that has a date, assignments, exams, holidays, after school activities, doctor appointments, dental appointments, all go on the calendar.

Make sure your calendar is large enough to handle all the important information you may have on one day. Use a color coding system to ensure that the important dates are all circled in BIG RED MARKER! Make sure that you use red as the color for urgent things to be completed, like homework or project deadlines. Get in the habit of writing absolutely everything down. This habit of writing everything down will help you later in your career when you need to remember important dates.

Post your class schedule on your bulletin board so you know exactly what your next day's scheduled classes are, along with knowing what free periods you have in between classes.

Post the phone numbers of other students in your class. It is important to be able to contact other students if you get stuck on an assignment, or miss a class.

Keep on or near your desk:

- Tape

- Scissors

- Magic markers

- Pens

- Pencils

- Paper Clips

- Supply of extra notebook paper

- Supply of scrap paper

If you keep these things nearby and neatly in a box, drawer on a bookshelf, you won't have to search your whole room every time you need a pencil.

CHECK YOUR PENS AND PENCILS! Test them all and if they don't work throw them away!

Optional but handy items to keep near your desk:

- Dictionary

- Thesaurus

- Library card

- Watch or clock

Buy a binder and separate notes for each subject with a divider. Look for binders that have sleeves to hold handouts. Keep an extra copy of your class schedule taped to the inside cover of your binder.

 Keep Track of Assignments. Copy all of your assignments into a special assignment pad and then copy them onto your wall calendar. This way you won't forget or lose track of assignments.

PLACES TO STUDY BESIDES YOUR DESK

When it's time to study we often need a change of scenery to be able to concentrate and yet we want to ensure that activities of others don't distract us. Sometimes a different atmosphere gives us a boost of energy and further enhances our study time by making it more enjoyable simply by being away from the usual routine of school and home.

The library is often the best place to study for many reasons. They maintain a code of silence, so that makes for a better venue than most, plus you have access to unlimited resources if you need to do any research whether online or in the reference materials readily available in this location. You might do this with a study group or by yourself, making it a wonderful alternative.

A bookstore is also a good place to study as they often have quiet corners with tables and chairs. It also gives you access to more resources; should you get stuck on something you can always get help. A coffee shop such as Starbucks or other chains offer online access and have comfortable chairs and tables in quiet corners where you can wile away the hours with a cup of coffee to keep you company. Watch out for Internet access though! Having Internet access may not be an advantage to studying as there are so many distractions online.

A park is a wonderful alternative study place because there are benches that you can sit on or you can bring a blanket and stretch out on it under a tree out of the way of people playing so that you can enjoy your solitude out in the fresh air and sunshine. An Internet café is another place that offers you the opportunity to study or do research online with other people who are doing similar activities. Any of these offer good alternatives so that you break up the boredom of regular routine and do something more stimulating that does not deter your studying.

PLACES TO AVOID WHEN TRYING TO STUDY

This might seem like a silly topic because everyone should know where they should not go when they want to study. After all – you're not entirely stupid, right? However, it's not a question of stupid – it's more a question of what is practical and the reality of what usually happens.

When you come home from class, you might go to your room to study or do your homework. And while that is not entirely a bad idea because you probably have a desk in your room, there is also a bed -- and many students will promptly lie down and decide to study on the bed. This is a bad idea because the minute your head hits the pillow you will likely be fast asleep.

A living room or common room are not a good place as there will be constant interruptions and likely people watching television, talking and generally disturbing your study time. The kitchen may not be a good place to study. Even if you are at a table, you will have distractions with people coming and going. Either of these places will disrupt your study and impair your ability to absorb what you are studying.

Some people might think a mall will be all right because there are generally benches or chairs where you can sit, but the constant flow of people will be a distraction that you will not be able to avoid.

OK – so that's a little much – how about going to my friend's house and we can study together? This will offer the same distractions as your own home but you will have another person who will disturb your thoughts and probably end spending time talking, and socializing.

Like it or not, the best places to study are those where you have more isolation and less distraction – the library or the desk in your room (if you can avoid the bed) – offer the best solutions.

Pros And Cons Of Studying In A Coffee Shop

You've seen them, you've talked to them–but are you one of them? I'm talking about those people at the local coffee shop, who have their laptop computers and perhaps a textbook or two, along with their notebook and pen. I'm talking about the coffee shop studier. This is the person who, rather than going to the library or staying at home or in the dorm, they head to Starbucks or some other coffee shop to fill their brain with the material from their classes.

Studying at coffee houses is all the rage these days. But is it smart?

Why Study In A Coffee Shop?

Let's look at the main reasons why people take their studies to the coffee house, and then offer our own pros and cons for your study skills. Here are a few good reasons to study in a coffee shop:

It's a quiet, calm environment, similar to what you'd find at a library. But at a library, you'll sometimes run into friends and spend time visiting with them. That happens less often at a coffee shop.

For some people, a drink and a snack help them with the study process, and they're readily available at a coffee shop. Again, this isn't usually the case at the library (although some libraries are now experimenting with offering beverages).

Speaking of beverages, studying and caffeine go together like peanut butter and jelly. And you can't find a better source of caffeine than your local coffee house.

If you WANT to study with friends, it's easier to do so at a coffee house than at the library, because there are usually couches for groups, and there's no librarian "shushing" you when you start talking.

And finally, more and more coffee houses have outside sitting–perfect for when the weather is nice and you'd prefer to be studying outside.

Coffee Shop Studying Is Good For Some People – Others – Not So Much

1. Most people need a quiet place to study, and so a library or coffee shop – either one will work for this purpose.

2. However, libraries usually limit the amount of time you can be on the Internet. Generally, coffee houses do not, so if you need more online time, the coffee shop is the better choice.

3. On the other hand, if you need an all-day study session, the folks at the library are less likely to mind

you staying around without paying than the people at Starbucks. So if you can't afford to keep buying items but need to study all day, a library is a better choice than a coffee shop.

4. Finally, if you need absolute silence, go to the library. If you need more freedom to talk to people, such as your "study buddies," a coffee house works better.

GET THE MOST OUT OF COFFEE-HOUSE STUDY SESSIONS:

Go at times when it's not likely to be as busy. It's no fun getting there at the breakfast or lunch rush only to find that there's no table available.

If you're with a group, head for the couch, if they have one. You can squeeze more of your friends there than at one of those tiny tables. Plus it's more comfortable for those long study sessions.

Don't spend any more time on the Internet than necessary. It's too easy to be distracted by email, instant messages, and random surfing. First, do as much study without the Internet as possible, saving the online work for last.

Finally, remember to buy something at least every couple of hours. This way, the staff who work there won't get irritated that you're taking up space, and you won't be made to feel awkward.

PREPARING A STUDY SCHEDULE

It's important when devising a study schedule to start by organizing your schedule into a table or chart that shows all your classes and regular appointments for each week. There should be a space to write your class timetable for each day and an area to keep track of practices, meetings and regular appointments.

Once your table is set up, you can make a space for each subject and designate a time to study for each one. Use a highlighter if that helps it stand out and keep you organized.

The biggest challenge when preparing a study schedule is often deciding which subject to study first. Ranking your study period can take practice.

Start with subjects you need to be prepared for the next day. Then figure out about how long it will take you to complete assignments and plan your study time around that schedule. If you have a big project coming up, spread out the assignment throughout your study week.

If you take the time to figure out a study schedule, you can free up more of your time during the week. And you won't stress over cramming at the last minute for a test or lose sleep over pulling an all-nighter. If you organize your time, you'll figure out there's time to study as well as do things you enjoy. You won't have to feel guilty over slacking off or sick to your stomach that you won't do well on a test.

ORGANIZATION TIPS

Keeping yourself organized

By keeping a study schedule you keep yourself organized and allow yourself to get more work done in a shorter period of time (which frees up more time to do what you want.) Make sure when you organize your schedule that you allot enough time for each subject. Organize your time so that your focus allows more time for the subjects you find most difficult. Don't ignore any subject, but rank your time so you can improve on the ones that give you the most grief.

Don't be afraid to switch your study schedule up a bit if things aren't working for you. If you need to spend more time on a particular subject, rearrange your schedule to match your current priorities. And give yourself a little breathing room in that schedule. Although you want to follow the schedule faithfully, everyone needs to allow for a little flexibility in their schedule.

The purpose of your schedule is not to lock down all your time!

DON'T WASTE TIME

Make sure you don't get in the habit of wasting time. It's important to organize your study time with other commitments, like jobs or sports practices. Take advantage of every spare minute of the day, and don't slack off. If you get to class a few minutes early, spend that time reviewing your work. Get in the habit of bringing your books with you so you can study during the day, like when you're waiting for the bus, or while dinner is cooking. Fold your notes and put them in your pocket so you have easy access to them when a few minutes of study time pop up in the day.

Using every minute to study sounds like you have to work all the time. Not quite! If you make use of spare moments, then you free up time and get things done faster. Then you have more time left over to do what you want!

This is the whole goal - make use of unproductive time, like waiting for the bus, to study and then you have more free time in the evening. Flash cards are a great way to study at odd moments and we will talk about them later.

Create a daily study schedule

Although a weekly study schedule is an excellent way to keep you organized, you can also use other types of schedules such as a daily schedule. This can be as simple as writing out a list of things you need to do, in the order they need to be done, at the start of each day. There's something to be said about writing a task down; it makes it more definite. This daily schedule can complement your weekly schedule, which will refer to your monthly, term and yearly schedule. Keeping an eye on the daily details as well as your long-term goals can keep you organized and lead to success.

How to Make a Study Plan - The Complete Guide

Getting Organized!

While it is tough to make studying fun, it is entirely possible to make it simple, effective and totally worth your while.

Getting organized allows you to study less, get better marks AND have more time for other things. To gain the maximum benefit from your study sessions, there are few key points you can follow.

For most students, the most difficult part of any exam is the actual studying. Typically, there is so much material to study that students begin to procrastinate, putting off studying until the night before. After a late-night cram session, students arrive at the exam tired and feeling dazed by the sheer amount of information they've tried to absorb. The easiest way to study for an exam, and avoid the cram sessions, is to make a study plan.

Time – There are two time elements that are crucial to an effective study plan. The first time element to consider is how much time you have until the exam, while the second is the amount of time each day that you can set aside for studying.

Try to study for at least two hours per day for major exams, like entrance exams, and at least thirty minutes per day for lecture exams. If you are limited on the amount of time until the exam, such as one week or less, then you will need to increase your daily study time. Set up a schedule with clearly marked study times for each day.

Content – The content to be studied depends on the type of exam. For placement exams, entrance exams, and licensure exams, there are no specific textbooks or prior lecture notes. There are, however, commercially available review guides, and textbooks and lecture notes from past classes often contain a great deal of material that will help with the exam. By looking at the content areas of the test, you can determine what readily available material to study. For course-based exams, textbooks and lecture notes are both ideal study content. Break the content into chunks, and then assign specific chunks to the study times that you have listed on your schedule.

For most College courses, the table of contents of the course textbooks, as well as the course outline give a structured overview of what you need to study for an exam. Xerox the textbook table of contents, and then integrate that with the course outline and your schedule. Check off the areas that you know well and highlight the areas that you need to spend time on. Estimate the time required to study your weak areas, and then portion out what you need to study into the time available to study and mark it on your calendar.

Here are a few more tips for organizing course material into a study plan:

> **Chronological** – Assign chunks of material to study times in chronological order. In other words, study the material in the order that it was presented. Remember to allot more time for studying the most important information.

> **Critical first** – Assign study times so the most critical method is covered first, and then work down to the least important information. Allow more time for covering the most critical information. If you are having trouble with the most important information, re-assign time from the least important information.

THE BEST STUDY PLAN – START EARLY AND STUDY REGULARLY

Never leave your studying until the last minute. Not only will it be incredibly stressful, but it will also be ineffective and your results will be disappointing. Make studying part of your daily routine. This may be difficult at first. Start off with short study sessions and gradually increase the time. Work your way up to 45 minutes, which is ideal for most people. Take a break, then back for more.

Make the Time – You have the time (or can make the time). How to use daily routine to study   Instead of not having the time, it's more likely that you don't want to, or it isn't a priority. Studying needs to become a priority. Sure, exercise, a social life and some personal down time are integral to your overall health and well-being, but placing studying a little further up the list won't hurt you. If you are genuinely busy (as many students are), here are some tips on how to add study time to your already busy schedule:

• **Prioritize** – relaxing in front of Netflix may sound more appealing than hitting the books, but if you really want to see academic results, your studies need to come first. It is always helpful to write your priorities down as a visual reminder. Try making a few points on a sticky note and put it by the bathroom mirror – that way you will be constantly reminded of the important tasks you must complete.

• **Delegate** – if you have some jobs that need to get done, see if any of them can be delegated to someone else. Perhaps your house mate can do the groceries this week, maybe a sibling can baby sit your niece instead, or the co-captain can organize this week's team sheet. Look through your list of jobs and responsibilities to see if any can be permanently delegated so you focus on your studies. Delegating goes hand in hand with prioritizing, put your studies first and other tasks second.

You don't have to give jobs away permanently. See if you can get someone to take over for you for a couple of weeks while you prepare for a big exam. Then take over for them.

Use Your Travel Time – if you use public transport, use it as study time. It may not be appropriate for writing extensive notes, but reading through your existing notes will be helpful. You could also record your notes and listen to them to provide variety in your study. This may also be useful if you drive, instead of listening to the radio, listen to your revision notes.

You will most likely find a whole heap of time available to you that you have never considered before. Organize study tasks that you can do riding the bus or train and prepare for your commute. Use your Daily Routine

Use Class Time – this may sound confusing, isn't class time for learning new material? Sure it is, but by paying more attention in class and completing set tasks in class time, you will make your study time at home more effective. If you already understand the content and have asked your teacher questions, you will be able to get on with revising or studying other, more difficult, subjects. If you treat your class time like a social event, your initial study time will be spent trying to understand what has already been explained to you. When you are home alone, you don't have the opportunity to clarify things with your teacher or ask them to help you.

Use your Daily Routine

The Waiting Game: Making Use Of Your Daily Routine

One of the main concerns students have: not having enough time in a day to complete everything they need to. Students do not realize that they have several breaks in their day that they can use more effectively. They also do not realize how much time they spend playing "the waiting game": waiting in line or waiting for something else to be finished before they will resume studying. By using these "breaks" more effectively, they can give themselves real breaks and still have time for social life and sleep.

Commute

Students commute to class anywhere from 5 minutes to an hour. Usually there is a long wait time for the bus: they could use that time, and the time spent on the bus, to review their readings, listen to audio recordings, or review pre-written flashcards. Even if the bus is noisy, it will test their concentration skills and how they react under pressure.

Exercise

Students generally find it difficult to balance a healthy lifestyle with their studies. Depending on the workout, they can incorporate some time to study. Treadmills and ellipticals have a flat table surface on them: students can use this to put their notebook on and review their notes while they do some cardio.

Phones

Students spend a lot of time on their phones. By downloading flashcard apps they can use their phones more effectively. They could also watch youtube videos on a given subject.

Meal Prepping

Meal prepping requires a lot of planning and time spent waiting for meals to cook. Students generally opt for quick meals such as pasta or rice. Both of these meals require waiting for water to boil then waiting for the food to cook. Students can use this time to pull out their flashcards or review their readings.

Laundry

Students dread doing their laundry: it consumes too much of their time and they spend most of it procrastinating, while waiting for it to finish. Students can bring their books or flashcards to the laundry room. Students usually set a timer for when the laundry is done; they can use this time to complete a mock test and see how well they perform or how much they know during the limited amount of time.

Waiting in line

Students generally need their coffee or snack fix while studying. The wait times on and off campus stretch out the door. By the time they go to order 15 minutes has gone by. Students should bring their flashcards, paper or electronic, to pass the time and utilize their study time. Coffee shops are generally loud and chaotic, which will also test the students concentration skills.

Students always find themselves in a time-crunch. Once they realize they can incorporate studying into their daily routine without cutting into their social life or sleep schedule they will reduce their stress and notice an improvement in their academic results. Thus, "the waiting game" does not have to be a waste of time or an excuse to procrastinate.

Student tip

Made a study plan more than a month in advance.

I ended up not following it at all. Why? Because I had made it so far in advance, it didn't take into account assignments and tests our teachers gave us in the month before The Exams. Another issue was that I had actually retained a fair amount of what I had meant to study in some areas, and struggled excessively with the material in other areas.

On Study Plans:

When you make a study plan, a) make sure you actually have time to everything you meant to do (so don't do it too far in advance) and b) keep the plan flexible. If I already knew something, it was very tempting to just use the time I'd allotted to instead procrastinate. If I was having trouble with something, I ended up cutting myself short in order to stay within the time I'd allotted.

What worked for me was making a goal to study x number of units in each of my subjects within a week. Not a day. A week. This gave me the flexibility to spend as much time as I needed (or didn't need) on each unit, while still keeping me somewhat organized.

This might not work for you! Maybe you need more structure! If you're still at a point where your grades don't really matter yet, don't act like me and not take school seriously! (more exclamation marks!!!) This is the time to figure out what will work for you and what won't. You do NOT want to be in a position where your marks do matter, and you can't figure out how you best study. Again, find what works for you. There are lots of resources for ways to study.

SIX KEY POINTS FOR YOUR STUDY PLAN:

1. GATHER SUPPLIES

This step is the simplest of them all. Check out the local stationary store and equip yourself with supplies. Colored pens, highlighters, calendars, planners and sticky notes all make wonderful additions to your planning process. These days, the calendar on your phone is a useful tool. You always have it with you so start storing your appointments, exams, events so you can clearly see when you have spare time. There are also plenty of apps that will help plan your study schedule and track your progress.

2. SET EDUCATIONAL GOALS

Having clear goals is essential to staying motivated. In high school, this may be getting accepted into a certain college. Know what subjects and results are required, write them down, and factor them into your study plan. In other words, focus your time on the subjects that will help you qualify for your preferred college. If you are already in college, you may be looking for a scholarship or internship where certain results are needed.

3. DESIGN YOUR STUDY SCHEDULE BASED ON A WEEKLY TIME FRAME

It's not a bad thing to be focused on the future. Plan too far ahead and you lose sight of what is important right now. Also, priorities change, appointments get made, and unexpected events pop-up. By planning weekly you can be flexible, make changes based on the results of the previous week, and plan for all your needs. Longer term plans become unwieldy the farther events are from the present.

Try to keep some study sessions the same from week to week. This helps you get into a routine. Where possible, schedule certain subjects the evening after you attended the class. You will have the information fresh in your mind and more likely to be committed to your long-term memory.

If possible, review notes from the days class on that day. See our post on taking better notes

4. USE TO-DO LISTS

A 'to-do' list is a valuable supplement to your study schedule. Keep an area free in your notebook for your 'to-do' list. This allows for any extra study that crops up at the last minute (keep in mind that your study schedule is made in advance, so this is bound to happen). You may have all your study sessions accounted for when your chemistry teacher issues a last-minute assignment due in two days. This assignment will be added to your 'to-do' list and scheduled for an appropriate time. Try not to bump other subjects, instead always leave a bit of free time for these occasions – if nothing comes up at the last minute, you can have a well-deserved rest! Getting organized and staying organized will reduce stress

The to-do list is the raw material that feeds into your study schedule.

5. EVALUATE AND MAKE CHANGES

Don't worry if your study plan doesn't feel right at first. It may take time to figure out what works best for you. At the end of each week spend some time reflecting on your study plan. Make a note of what worked well and where some improvements can be made. For example, you may notice that there are certain times in the week when you are able to focus more and therefore use this time for more pressing or difficult subjects. You may have miscalculated your energy levels after a busy day and find that you are unable to focus and therefore this time might be best spent relaxing or reading over some low key notes. Try to evaluate not only at the end of each week, but also each night. A nightly evaluation will help ensure that you can fit everything into the week that you need, particularly if you need to do some rearranging due to last minute tests or assignments.

6. MAKE TIME FOR YOURSELF

Studying and academic success are important, but your personal health and well-being are even more so. Take time to exercise, socialize, relax and enjoy different activities. By doing these things you will improve your concentration levels and make your study time more effective.

STUDENT TIP

Grades on Fleek in One Week: A College Student's Study Guide

During my first year of college, a professor told me that preparing for a test should consist of at least 12 hours of review. I was shocked by his suggestion because I thought I spent a reasonable amount of time studying and had some A grades to show for it.

However, I began to change my study habits and found the results were noticeable. The time I use to spend preparing for a test had doubled and my average increased by six per cent. Now, I am grateful for his advice and follow a seven-day study method that has greatly improved my test scores.

Day 1: Achieve Notebook Goals

Fingers crossed that your favorite prof has provided you with an outline of what will be covered on the test. If not, resist becoming salty and get ready to work. You can prepare for the week ahead by collecting notes you have written since your course began or the previous test. Use either guideline to decide what notes include significant information or techniques that you need to review. Next, get creative with some hi-lighters or download a free flashcard App to ensure essential information is easily accessible. This will also make the things you need to know appear fresh to your eyes and excite your brain.

Suggested time: 2 Hours

Day 2: The Text is Blessed (With Useful Information)

Don't panic if you've been scrolling through Instagram rather than reading textbook chapters. Although I recommend reading chapters (and taking notes) as they are assigned, scanning the sections you have neglected can be helpful. Skim-read the pages to find sentences that are similar to the ones in your lecture notes and read the surrounding paragraphs to discover supporting information. You are likely to find the answer to a test-question that was not discussed in-depth during your lecture.

Suggested time: 2 Hours

Day 3: Get Woke

Remember the sentences in your textbook that you ignored because you had no idea what they meant? Now is the time to get lit with knowledge by finding definitions and examples that provide clarity. Use the internet, a dictionary or your fellow classmates to help you decode each puzzling word or phrase. Finding solutions independently or with a team is a fantastic way to increase your sense of fierceness and bring out your inner Scantron warrior.

Suggested time: 1 Hour

Day 4: Story Replay

Look through the required pages of your textbook a second time to enhance your expertise. I highly recommend turning off your phone during this two-hour session in order to stay focused. If you get bored, try reading out loud to yourself, a roommate or even a puppy who's cuteness won't distract you (impossible, right?). This may sound silly but being engaged decreases the chances of becoming side-tracked and makes it more likely that you retain useful information. How to Study from Textbooks

Suggested time: 2 Hours

Day 5: Leg Day

Get ready for some ah-ha! moments during the study equivalent to leg day. Even if the material seems repetitive, it is important to push through day five if you want to ace your test. Spend these two hours learning the information you hilighted or transferred onto flashcards. This is an important chance to connect the information you found in your textbook to your upgraded lecture notes. Relating information from both sources can help you give detailed answers to challenging questions on your test.

Suggested time: 2 Hours

Day 6: Schedule Delivery

Use the promise of delicious pizza to convince a friend to be your study aid. Your partner doesn't have to have any previous subject knowledge, but they do need to have good taste in pizza toppings. When you meet up, choose one person to act as the professor who will either deliver the mock-test (study aid) or give a lecture on the subject matter (test taker). Acting out either scenario will add enough pressure to put you in test-mode and achieve expert status.

Suggested time: 3 Hours & A Pizza Break

Day 7: No Stress

The day before your test is all about chillin'. You are encouraged to put your books away until after your test and do something that relaxes you. Choose low-key activities like watching Netflix or making the dessert from that video you bookmarked a month ago. Then, end the day with a goodnight's sleep to make sure you can think clearly during your test. Now that your study plan is complete, you should feel like brushing them shoulders off and finessin' through the testin'.

Suggested time: All Day

This study method comes from a long history of reliable study habits and consistent academic achievements. I graduated from the program that wise professor taught me in as the highest ranked graduate at the top of my class. Today, enrolled in college for the second time, I still use this study method to maintain honour roll status and an above-average GPA. If you want to improve your test scores, I suggest giving this seven-day study plan a try. I can confirm that it can be worked into a packed schedule and completed in only one week. In other words, put your grades on fleek in the same amount of time it takes to binge-watch a murder docu-series and even have time to finish season two.

GENERAL TIPS

Now that you have your study plan and schedule in place, there are a few final tips to make your study session even more valuable.

START IMMEDIATELY

Do not leave all your study until the last minute. Keep on top of it, your weekly schedule will help with this. Make study notes each week and when the time comes to revise you will have done most of the hard work. This means you will actually be able to spend your time revising rather than learning the content.

SUBJECT ORDER

If you find yourself studying your favorite subject first, and spending more time doing so, you could be getting into trouble. You're better off starting with subjects that you struggle with or do not particularly enjoy first. By getting them done first, you are studying your most difficult subjects when your concentration levels are at their highest, and you are avoiding accidentally missing them entirely. Try varying your subject study order to keep things interesting.

BUILD UP STUDY TIME

Don't get too ambitious and plan to study the same topic for one whole hour. Start with 20 minutes blocks and slowly build up from there.

A STUDY PLAN WILL HELP YOU ACHIEVE YOUR ACADEMIC GOALS RELATIVELY STRESS-FREE.

It may take some time to master a schedule that works best for you so stick with it. Make changes when you need to and adapt to suit your learning style, educational goals, extra-curricular activities and so on. The most important thing to remember is to create your schedule on a weekly basis and let it become part of your routine.

ASSESS YOURSELF

What don't you know?

The first step is to assess your strengths and weaknesses. You may already have an idea of where your weaknesses are, or you can take our Self-assessment modules for each of the content areas.

Exam Component	Rate 1 to 5
Reading Comprehension	
Paragraph & Passage Comprehension	
Drawing inferences & conclusions	
English (optional)	
Punctuation (Optional)	
English Grammar (Optional)	
Math	
Metric Conversion	
Algebra	
Fractions	
Decimals	
Percent	

The key to making a study plan is to divide the material you need to learn into manageable sized pieces and learn it, while at the same time reviewing the material that you already know.

Using the table above, any scores of 3 or below, you need to spend time learning, going over and practicing this subject area. A score of 4 means you need to review the material, but you don't have to spend time re-learning. A score of 5 and you are OK with just an occasional review before the exam.

A score of 0 or 1 means you really need to work on this should allocate the most time and the highest priority. Some students prefer a 5-day plan and others a 10-day plan.   It also depends on how much time you have until the exam.

A score of 0 or 1 means you really need to work on this area and should allocate the most time and the highest priority. Some students prefer a 5-day plan and others a 10-day plan. It also depends on how much time you have until the exam.

Here is an example of a 5-day plan based on an example from the table above:

> **Fractions:** 1 Study 1 hour everyday – review on last day
> **Punctuation:** 3 Study 1 hour for 2 days then ½ hour a day, then review
> **Percent:** 4 Review every second day
> **Word Problems:** 2 Study 1 hour on the first day – then ½ hour everyday
> **Reading Comprehension:** 5 Review for ½ hour every other day
> **Algebra:** 5 Review for ½ hour every other day
> **Grammar:** 5 very confident – review a few times.

Using this example, Algebra and Grammar are good and only need occasional review. Punctuation is also good and needs 'some' review. Decimals need a bit of work, Word Problems need a lot of work and Fractions are very weak and need the majority of time. Based on this, here is a sample study plan:

Day	Subject	Time
Monday		
Study	Fractions	1 hour
Study	Word Problems	1 hour
	½ hour break	
Study	Punctuation	1 hour
Review	Grammar	½ hour
Tuesday		
Study	Fractions	1 hour
Study	Word Problems	½ hour
	½ hour break	
Study	Decimals	½ hour
Review	Percent	½ hour
Review	Grammar	½ hour
Wednesday		
Study	Fractions	1 hour
Study	Word Problems	½ hour
	½ hour break	
Study	Punctuation	½ hour
Review	Grammar	½ hour
Thursday		
Study	Fractions	½ hour
Study	Word Problems	½ hour
Review	Punctuation	½ hour
	½ hour break	
Review	Grammar	½ hour
Review	Percent	½ hour

Friday		
Review	Fractions	½ hour
Review	Word Problems	½ hour
Review	Punctuation	½ hour
	½ hour break	
Review	Percent	½ hour
Review	Grammar	½ hour

READING

TEXTBOOKS AND OTHER COURSE MATERIALS

The main reason studying can be difficult is the massive amounts of reading required by just about every class you take. It is an inevitable part of being a student. Why is reading so difficult for some? Well, it can be time consuming and feel like work, especially when you don't particularly like the subject matter that you have to read or if you have copious amounts of reading and not a lot of time to finish.

But difficulty with reading doesn't have to stop you from making good grades if you know the tricks to getting through page after page in an efficient way. Here are some dos and don'ts for getting reading done when time isn't on your side.

READING DO'S AND DON'TS

Reading Do's

Break up pages into 20, 40, 60 or 80-page sections. For example, If you are given an assignment on Monday to read 4 chapters of your biology book by Wednesday, then make a plan to read two chapters that afternoon and two chapters on Tuesday. You don't have to get through all it at once.

Always take breaks while reading. If it's 6 p.m. and you have to read 200 pages by morning, read in 40-page increments and take 10- to 15-minute breaks. Turn on the TV for a few minutes or walk the dog. Make sure to limit yourself to the time planned. Don't get trapped by the TV or other distractions!

Know your reading speed! It's a good idea to know how long it takes you to read a page of text. Read five pages and time yourself. Then, multiply that by how many pages you have to read. This will give you a good sense of how long it will take you to read your assignment.

Reading Don'ts

Don't read in bed. Your bed is where you sleep. It's a place you go for relaxation and rest. You are far more likely to "nod off" or become too tired to read if you are reclining or lying down in a place that your body and mind usually associate with sleep. Try sitting on a flight of stairs, or upright in a chair in your living room. Go to the park and sit on a bench to read, so long as you are not distracted by everyone and everything around you.

Don't forget to stay hydrated. OK, OK ... you're not running a marathon, but it's still important to take care of your body while reading. Sip some water, make a cup of tea or coffee on one of your breaks. But, be wary of too much caffeine because it can have a tendency to make your mind wander.

With these do's and don'ts you will certainly be on your way to developing smarter choices for completing massive amounts of reading. It's all about time management, and it doesn't always have to feel like work.

READING STRATEGIES

It's worth it to do a little extra reading in a subject. Your study notes will have more meaning if you are more familiar with the subject. You can elaborate on what you have learned in class, and it will not only allow you to do well in class it will also carry on into your future education.

When you read notes make sure you adjust the speed of your reading to the material you are reading. You can read a sports article a lot faster than a history textbook. A book you read for pleasure is a lot different than an essay in which you need to remember specific facts.

Here are some reading strategies that will help you read faster and retain more:

Don't mouth the words.

When you read, don't get into the bad habit of mouthing the words as you go along. This will slow you down. It is OK to do this once in a while, if you are trying to understand an unfamiliar arrangement of words, but for the most part, it's a reading technique that reduces the speed.

Think about what you are reading

Make sure when you are reading you are actually taking in the information and are not just running your eyes along the words. Be an active thinker while you read. Stop occasionally to take in what you are reading. See if you can answer questions about the text like:

- Does the author know what he is talking about?

- What is the point of this?

- Am I convinced that this person is right?

- Who did the author write this piece for?

- When was this information written and when was it published?

Scan a section before you read it

It's a good idea to scan a long section of writing before reading it. You might decide that the particular passage can be read quickly and doesn't have to be intensively read. On the other hand you may want to re-read certain sections of a chapter that are particularly important.

Whenever you read a textbook assignment, remember to always read the title, the subtitle and the table of contents. This will give you an overview of the content. See if you can turn the title into a question and try to answer it from the information you learned in the previous chapter.

Once you've finished a chapter, review it by asking yourself questions about the information. Come up with your own tests and see how you do. It will give you an idea about how much of the information you understand, and how much you will need to study.

Pay attention to visuals

It's important, while you're reading chapters, to pay attention to graphs, tables and illustrations. There's often a lot of information in tables and charts and it is an easy way to memorize important facts. Sometimes, however, the illustrations are a waste of time. Don't get side tracked.

CHANGING YOUR READING SPEED

Reading for different purposes means adjusting your reading rate.

- Why are you reading?

- To get the general idea?

- To learn, point by point, in detail?

- To find one particular point or fact in something you've already read?

- To entertain yourself?

- What type of material are you reading?

- How difficulty of the material for you?

- Is it easy?

- Is it difficult?

- How familiar are you with the subject?

- Do you have some background on the subject?

- Is it totally new?

Reading efficiently means changing your reading speed as often as required.

For example, say you are reading a science book about Mars. At the beginning, there is a short story about exploring Mars. You can read this very quickly. After the story, there is information about the chemistry of the Martian surface. Slow down and read carefully. Or, you may not be interested in the chemistry at all, so you can skim this part or skip it completely.

If you are reading this book to find out about NASA exploration of Mars, you can skim the first two sections until you get to the section on NASA exploration.

What is your purpose? Depending on why you are reading your speed will change.

Purpose	Speed
Reading for main idea only	Fast
Reading for fun	Fast
Reading to learn new material	Slow
Find a fact or idea	Fast
Reading as 'art' e.g. poetry	Slow

What kind of material are you reading? Depending on the type of material, your speed will change.

Purpose	Speed
Difficult Vocabulary and ideas	Slow
Subjects you already know	Fast
Technical reading	Slow
Instructions or Directions	Slow

Certain words are clues, for you to either speed up or slow down your reading speed.

Speed up signals

• Any passage with no vocabulary blocks, no complicated sentences or ideas.

• A passage where you only want the most important idea. A passage that repeats or elaborates on something you already know.

• A passage that gives examples of something you already know.

• A passage about something you already know a lot about.

• A passage that is not related to your purpose in reading.

Slow down signals

• New or difficult vocabulary or ideas.

• Details you want to remember.

• Subjects that are new to you.

• Directions that you need to follow exactly.

• Reading that refers to a picture or diagram where you have to shift back and forth between the reading and the diagram.

READING STRATEGY FOR TEXTBOOKS

One of the most painful things you'll do when you first start a new class is to buy the textbooks. Advance warning: they ain't cheap. You're going to hate plunking down $50, $100, even $150 for books for one class. Try not to hold a grudge too long. You need to quickly develop a real respect for textbooks. For a couple of reasons. First, because textbooks are written by some of the sharpest minds in their field. This means that your textbook is the best path to learning the material that comprises your college education. And more immediately, it's likely that your instructor will pull a lot of exam material from the text. This means your textbook becomes an important key to making an "A."

A few suggestions on showing respect to your textbooks and getting the most from them:

Take it slow. Numerous studies show that reading fast lowers your comprehension. If you're going to zip through the chapter as fast as possible, then don't waste your time. Go out for pizza or watch a movie. You'll probably learn just as much. But when you get serious about learning the material in the textbook, sit down with no interruptions and read for comprehension rather than for speed.

Read it more than once. You know how when you see a movie two or three times, you always catch things you never caught the first time? The same thing happens with textbooks. Each time you read it, something new will click in your brain and you'll learn something else.

Don't skip passages. What happens often is that a student will see a part that he feels is going to be especially boring, and he'll either not read that section or speed through it real fast. Unfortunately, it's often these difficult parts that an instructor often uses for a large part of the exam. As much as you might hate to hear this, it's probably a good idea to study those parts that you hate more and longer.

Practice active reading. Passive reading is where you just read the words and hope that the meaning of the words sinks into your brain. Active reading is more interactive.

One of the most important strategies in active reading is writing down notes as you read. Most textbooks will have space in the margins for this so that your notes of what you think is important are visually connected with the material itself. If the margins are too small, though, then you should still take notes in a notebook, while also highlighting the relevant points in the textbook itself. Writing down information makes it more likely that you'll remember the material.

Another active-reading strategy is that of asking yourself questions. Try to anticipate questions that might be on the exam. Then write these close to the material in your textbook. Use a pencil, if possible, so you can erase if necessary.

Keep your textbook in good shape. This means to keep the cover clean. Don't bend back the cover or dog-ear the pages. There are two good reasons for this. First, on a psychological level, you will value those things that you keep in good shape (and disregard things that your brain considers without value). A second reason is that, when the course is done, you might want to sell the textbook. It will bring in more money if it's in good condition.

READING STRATEGY FOR NOVELS

Reading novels teaches us about different worlds, eras and people. For this reason, they are an integral part of getting educated. It's important not to be intimidated by the language and issues in novels; instead, practice strategies that help you navigate the text.

Pre-reading:

A little research - Research can be simple, like a keyword search that gives some information about the genre you are reading; the author; the time period in which the novel is set; or the subject matter of the book. These key words can generally be found on the back or inside cover of the book and will give the reader outside information to help understand the story. Research can also be more complex, like checking out a book from the library that has essays written about the novel.

Predict - Think ahead and try to predict the plot. Flip through the first section of the book and look for a short piece of dialogue or text. Predict what will happened. Revisit your thoughts when you get to that piece.

Essay questions – If you know you will be writing about the novel, begin thinking about possible topics and write them down. As you encounter potentially useful material during the book, add these to your notes.

While reading:

New words - Keep a list of the new words you encounter. Make a chart that includes a box for the word, its definition, how it's used in the book and the final box for your interpretation.

Visualize - Turn on the movie projector in your head. Take a minute during the action to visualize what is happening and what the characters look like.

Conflict - Most novels have conflict. A pictorial representation of the conflict will help you remember it and understand it better. Make a graph that has the six main conflicts (character vs. character, society, technology, self, supernatural and nature) at the top with space underneath. Write the conflict at the top and then pictures or stick figures demonstrating what's happening in the text. If you like to journal, write about it instead of drawing a picture.

Compare - Don't be afraid to compare the characters with yourself. What would you do in that situation? How might the story have turned out differently had the main or secondary character been you?

Quotations – You'll probably need to cite specific words from the novel in an essay, or maybe you'll just want to remember some meaningful phrases. Write down the quote or at least a few key words and the page number, so you can find it again easily. Highlight or underline the words in the book.

Post-reading:

Talk about it - Get a group together of other students who are reading the same book. By discussing the book you'll get a deeper understanding of what happened and what there is to learn from it. Keep a list of questions you had while you read and bring them to the group. If the conversation stops, have a "gossip session" discussing the characters; what's wrong with them and what they should have done differently.

Reread – go through and reread any section or part of the

novel that didn't turn out as you expected. Check the text for something you may have missed that made the ending unclear or confusing.

The most important part of reading a novel is to enjoy the process and the story. Always look for who and what you like about a story and keep a great attitude!

READING STRATEGY FOR ESSAYS

Essays can be a great source of information; these are especially popular since they come with the huge advantage of allowing you to choose the level of depth you would like to delve into the topic. Irrespective of how deep an author has preferred to go while covering a topic, by selecting portions that you deem necessary and ignoring other parts where there are intricate details, you can control the amount of information. However, to figure out exactly what to highlight and what you can ignore, it is necessary to analyze the essay first. There are a few easy steps that will enable you to do this quickly and efficiently.

The first of these is to skim through the entire essay once. Glance through the pertinent points that the essay covers and read through quickly to get an idea as to which part of the essay covers what. This will help you come straight to the portions that you would like to take excerpts from while using the essay.

It also helps to keep a pencil handy; this way you can highlight important sections. You can also mark words that you probably are not familiar with so that they can be looked up in a dictionary later. By the end of this brisk reading session, you will have a vague idea as to what the author has attempted to convey by the entire essay. At this point, vague is OK.

Next, take a more detailed look at the essay by reading through it more slowly and carefully. Take time to soak up the exact meaning of the different parts of the essay that you had highlighted earlier. Look up the unfamiliar words too; this is a great way to improve your vocabulary as well. It helps to make notes in your own words so that it becomes easier to assimilate the contents of the essay. Now comes the time to ponder the central underlying idea behind the essay – the thesis.

Once this is done, you are almost done with the elementary analysis of the essay, and any further variations of the central underlying theme can be explained using the analyst's personal style and flair. This general rule can be kept in mind to decipher the seemingly most complexly authored essays using the toughest of words that ever existed in any language. Using a structured approach such as the one mentioned above, it is possible to break the essay down into smaller and more easily comprehensible sections which can easily be understood.

HIGHLIGHTING

Marking in a college textbook helps you become an active learner and keeps your attention focused on the information in the text. There is a reason for this: Highlighting is an effective learning tool. And now, as you continue your education, if you want to improve your own study skills, you need to learn that highlighting is not just for nerds. If you'll give it a try, you'll be amazed at how it helps you remember that difficult material. Here are some suggestions regarding highlighting.

First, you need to create your own marking system. This must be a system which doesn't interfere with your textbook reading. Whereas a pencil can be used to jot down extra notes not specifically mentioned in the chapter, the highlighter's purpose is to immediately draw your eyes to important points already in the book. Your markings should be easily followed. You should work to highlight key phrases and points so that, when your eyes are drawn to the yellow, they are drawn to points that together, make an easy-to-follow outline of the chapter.

Remember that the highlighted portions in any chapter should be the exception rather than the rule. If you highlight everything, you highlight nothing. Think of it this way: If this entire article that you're reading was highlighted in yellow except this paragraph, where are your eyes drawn? That's right-

-they would be drawn to the part that is NOT highlighted. That's why it's so important that you highlight sparingly.

A good number to remember is 15--No more than 15% of a page should be highlighted. This means if your page has 50 lines of text, you should highlight no more than 7 or 8 lines.

You can also use your highlighter to emphasize graphs or diagrams that you think you need to know. However, rather than coloring the whole diagram yellow, simply draw a yellow line around the box.

One last suggestion: Consider using more than one color of highlighter. While yellow could be your default color for most points, you could use a different color (such as a light blue) for new vocabulary that you need to know.

These few suggestions will help you become more of an expert student--and add some color to your study time.

Student Tip

Colored Pens

When sitting in a dimly lit room watching a powerpoint on something you probably need to know for that test coming up, it can be hard to stay engaged. Especially when your teachers voice seems to just drone on and on. The ultimate hack for staying engaged (and getting the most fantastic study notes you've ever seen) is actually quite simple... Colored pens! Especially the gel ones, those things make your writing flow like water through that leak in the roof of the classroom. Colored pens make everything better! EVERY-THING. Color coding your notes not only helps make the lesson more interesting but has also been proven to improve your memory of the material. Plus, it's fun to write in colors, so you're bound to write down as much as possible!

TAKING NOTES

Put Note-Taking at the top of your study skills list. One of the key elements in passing any course is taking good notes. To learn the required information, your notes need to be thorough and organized in a way that makes them easy to review later. For many students, however, note taking is a difficult task, and often notes end with either too little or too much information, or the wrong information to make them useful.

Here are some strategies and tips to develop good note taking habits:

- **Prepare.** The first tip for taking better notes is to prepare for the lecture. Read over the assigned material before class. This will give you some familiarity with the material to be covered and allow you to formulate any questions about that material in advance. This will also help you take notes faster since it isn't the first time that you have heard about it.

- **Show up.** It's impossible to take great class notes if you don't go to class. Make sure you attend the first class because that's when the teacher will let you in on the course outline, and their expectations in terms of homework, class assignments and testing. You'll also get a good indication on how the course will be marked.

- **Keep showing up.** The best way to gather great notes for a class is to go to class every day. Aim for perfect attendance. Spending time with your teacher allows you to get to know her teaching style and allows you to better figure out what to study, and what the teacher is looking for in test answers. You may not actually make it to the end of the semester with perfect attendance, but if you shoot for perfect, then you have some room for the unexpected. This way you may have an attendance record of 98%, when you aimed for perfect. Nothing wrong with that!

• **Listen.** Taking good notes requires you to listen to the lecture. Listening to the lecture enables you to pick up on points that may not be covered in the written material for the class. And there will definitely be a lot of material that is only covered in the lectures. It also enables you to take better notes because you are able to hear the instructor say key words that help organize your notes. For example:

> • The instructor may emphasize certain points with tone, volume or gestures.

> • The instructor may use signal phrases like, "There are three reasons..." or "There are two points of view..." These phrases alert you to significant points and help you structure your notes.

> • The instructor may review at the start of class or summarize at the end, giving you a chance to make sure you have the most important points.

> • Often professors will actually tell you what is going to be on the final exam!

• **If you do miss a class** ... It's tough to miss a class, because the teacher is going to continue moving onto the next thing and you may have missed a crucial part of the course outline the day before. Any material mentioned in class is eligible to appear in a future test. If you do miss class, try to borrow notes from another student (one who takes good class notes).

• This is an excellent reason to exchange contact information with at least two other students in each of your classes on the first day. You never know when you'll need help catching up, and you don't want to wait until after you're in a tight spot.

• **Your notebook.** Don't underestimate the organizational power of your notebook. It's is the central location to arrange your class information in a way that is easiest for you to understand. Learn to take great study notes in your notebook and take care not to lose it!

• **Choosing a notebook.** The best type of notebook is a 3-ring binder type with loose-leaf paper.

• A loose-leaf binder notebook also allows you to remove old notes from the notebook to make it less cumbersome to carry around. Just remember to file your notes so that you can review them later, like for a final exam or a future course. Use a folder or an accordion filing system to keep old notes organized.

• **Stick to plain paper.** Some people prefer lined paper, others blank. Try them both and see what works for you. The best type of paper for taking notes is plain white paper. Your notes will show up clearer on plain, rather than colored paper.

• **Taking good study notes.** When taking study notes remember to write down just the main points of what is being said, and write it in whatever way you will be most likely to remember. These are your study notes, so there is no wrong way, while you understand it. We will go into quite a bit more detail about taking notes soon.

• **Dating and labeling your notes.** Get into the habit of writing the date and subject of your class on all your notes. It's critical for good organization and finding what you need later.

• **Identifying key words.** Keep an ear open for key words within a lecture. They will give you a hint as to the main focus of the class and hints on what is important to study.

- **Identifying main topics.** Once you have determined the main topic of a class, make note of it. Then you can start looking for the sub-topics. These topics should be well marked and underlined in your notes. Details on these topics discussed in class can be organized under these sections.

- **Write notes in your own words.** When writing notes, don't worry about copying exactly what your teacher says. It's best to write your notes in your own words. They will be easier for you to study from.

- **Write clearly.** The most important habit you can get into when taking notes in class it to write clearly – or clearly enough anyway. Notes don't have to be master-pieces, but on the other hand you have to be able to read them. If you can't read what you've written, your notes aren't going to be much good to you, and you don't want to waste your time re-writing all your class notes.

- **Don't use a laptop.** Unless you're an exceptionally fast touch typist who can structure notes effectively while typing and listening, this is probably not a great strategy. Laptops or handheld devices offer any number of potential distractions, like the temptation to go online, chat with friends, etc. It's best to turn off all electronic devices and keep your full focus on the class.

- **Don't waste time repeating facts.** You don't have to bother writing the same facts over and over again in your notes, even if your teacher tends to repeat a point. If the teacher repeats something, that is a sure sign it is important, but you don't have to write it down again - try underlining. Make sure you write as much down as you can, even if you feel like you understand it. You don't want to have to rely on your memory when it comes time for a test. It's best to have the facts down in your study notes so they can be reviewed, or clarified later.

• **Don't worry about complete sentences.** Don't worry about sentence structure or punctuation. Jot down notes in list or point form, with bullets, or in number form. Facts are easiest to study if they are listed in point form. Don't even try to write in paragraphs - you won't have time and will miss too much while trying to formulate paragraphs.

• **Listen for hints.** Keep your ears open for any hints on possible test questions. Many times a teacher will comment on the importance of information and infer, or actually say that the information will appear on an upcoming test. Make sure you highlight the information the instructor tells you is important. Take notes on any comments the teacher says about the material. She might indicate some material is more important than others, and some should be memorized sooner than others.

• **Find what works for you.** Find a style of note taking that works best for you. It doesn't matter if no one else can decipher what your abbreviations stand for, or what symbols mean. Since you can remember what it means, then your study notes are doing the trick.

• **Look over your notes regularly.** It's a good idea to read over your notes regularly, preferably within 24 hours and then on a regular schedule after that. Studies show this improves your retention and understanding of the material by a huge amount. If you put notes away until the end of the term, when you have to review for an exam, you might forget some of the details of a lesson from your notes alone. By regularly reviewing notes you can keep the main points fresh in your mind.

It's also a good idea to leave space at the end of your notes so you can add more material when it's time for review. See the Split Page and Cornell methods described below.

Organize your notes. Get in the habit of writing more detailed study notes from your class notes. You can elaborate on points made in a lecture when you've got more time, remembering to underline the main topic discussed in the class, as well as the sub-topics, and the key words. See the Cornell and Split Page methods below.

Extra reading. It's worth it to do a little extra reading in a subject. Your study notes will have more meaning if you take it upon yourself to read more on the subject. You can elaborate on what you have learned in class and it will not only allow you to do well in class, but also carry on into your future education.

Giving yourself clues. With practice you will become more skilled taking notes and will be able to write effective clues in your notes that will jog your memory to key facts and concepts. Study clues work as reminders to trigger a whole set of information. With practice you will know which clues work best for you.

STUDENT TIP

To make the most of your notes, you should remember two things. One, nobody else has to understand your notes, so you can make them sound as weird or inappropriate as possible if that is what allows you to remember your concepts better. You do not have to explain yourself to anyone else, so own your craziness. It only has to make sense to you. Two, the more outrageous, the better. You will remember something that is funny and wild a lot better than any dull notes. For me, adding swearing helps a lot. Studying does not need to be boring.

NOTE TAKING STYLES

Later in this chapter, we'll give you some sample documents to take notes on and in Appendix 3 there is a list of common abbreviations and symbols to learn and practice.

Taking notes is not a skill that comes naturally to many students and is not a skill that is taught in many classrooms. Most students just 'take notes' any way that strikes them without realizing there are many different styles. There is a wide variety of methods for taking good notes, and not all methods work for everyone.

Below are 5 different styles. Read them through and try them out - use one of them or develop your own style.

First, here's a detailed look at four common methods of note taking:

OUTLINE METHOD

The outline method of note taking is one that will probably look familiar.

The outline method starts on the left-hand side of the paper. The most important points are placed at the left edge of the paper. Less important points, which are typically ideas that support the main points, are indented to the right. Each set of less important points is indented more to the right. It is easy to see, at a glance, the level of importance of the different ideas because of the distance between them and the major points.

An alternate form, which requires a little more thought, is to start with minor points to the left and indenting as points get more important. The alternate outline form is best used in lectures where minor ideas are used to build up to the most important ideas.

With either form, indentation is enough to show the importance of the ideas and the relationship between them. If you would like something more concrete, however, you can opt for using dashes, bullets or a Roman numeral and letter combination for further emphasis. For the sake of speed and being able to focus on the lecture, you may want to consider adding the marks after class when you review your notes.

Outline notes look something like this:

I. First main topic

Subtopic
> 1. Detail
> 2. Detail

Subtopic
> 1. Detail
> 2. Detail

The outline method has several advantages. It not only shows the content and main points of the lecture, but also the relationship between points. With an outline, it is easy to identify the main points of the information, and reviewing can be as simple as turning main points into questions. In addition, the outline is set up so simply that it takes very little, if any, editing for notes to be easily understood.

A major benefit of the outline method is the ability to focus on the lecture. Outlining does not require speed or great detail, both of which take away from your ability to listen to what is said. Outlining does require that you pay enough attention to the lecture to be able to outline the key ideas, which can help you retain more of the information.

There are some disadvantages to the outlining method. It can be difficult to use in science and math courses because they are more about sequential relationships which outlining does not show. Courses with fast-paced lectures may also be difficult to outline, partially because outlining requires the note-taker to think about organization.

THE CORNELL METHOD

The first step to use the Cornell method is to divide your paper into three sections. About 2 inches from the bottom of your paper, draw a horizontal line all the way across the page. About 2.5 inches from the left side of your paper, draw a vertical line from the top to the horizontal line you have just drawn. On standard paper, this will give you a 2.5 x 9-inch section on the left, a 6 x 9-inch section on the right, and a 2 x 8.5-inch section at the bottom. It is important that you create all three sections because each section has its own purpose in the Cornell method.

Once you have divided your paper into three sections, you are ready to take notes. The 6 x 9-inch section is your note-taking section. This is where you begin the 6 R's of note taking.

1. **Record** – During the lecture, record your notes in the note-taking section. Just capture the main points. Grammar, punctuation and spelling are not vital, as long as you can read your notes later. You may want to develop your own shorthand or abbreviation method for your notes. Just be sure you can remember and understand them once you've left the classroom.

2. **Reduce** – After the lecture, reduce your notes to main keywords. These are cues to help you remember the information, and they are written in the 2.5-inch section to the left of the notes. The cue section is also a good place to note any questions that you have as you go over your notes.

3. **Summarize** – The summary of your notes goes in the 2-inch space at the bottom of the page. Summarize each page of notes at the bottom of that page. You can also summarize the entire lecture on the last page of the notes for that lecture. Most lists place recapitulation as the last step in the 6 R's, but it is best to write your summary after you write your cues in the left-hand column. Writing it immediately ensures that the information is still fresh in your mind, which helps you create a more accurate summary.

4. **Say it Back** – Actually saying it out loud can help to reinforce the learning process. Ideally, you can cover up the note-taking section and use the cue section to jog your memory when reciting.

5. **Reflect** – Think about your notes and the information that you have just learned. Consider how the information can be applied, and how it fits with what you already know. Figure out the significance of the information, and why knowing it is important.

6. **Review** – Review your notes frequently to keep from forgetting the information. If you set aside time several days each week to review and recite your notes, you will not have to worry about an all-night cram session before the exam.

Free Cornell Method Template

https://www.test-preparation.ca/pdf/Cornell-Method-Template.pdf

CORNELL NOTES EXAMPLE TEMPLATE

SPLIT-PAGE METHOD

The split-page method is exactly what it sounds like. You split the page by drawing a vertical line all the way down the paper. The line should be located 2.5 to 3 inches from the left-hand side of the paper.

So, what do you do with the two sides?

Similar to the Cornell method, the split-page method uses the right side of the divided page for recording lecture notes.

The left-hand side of the page can have one of two uses. Some students prefer to use the left column for writing down key-words from the notes or questions they may have about the material. This allows them to cover the notes and use only the keywords as prompts when reciting the information. If you use the left-hand column for cues and keywords, be sure to write them down when possible after the lecture, while the information is still fresh in your mind.

The more traditional use for the left side is creating an outline of the textbook by writing down keywords and main points, also known as the Outline method of taking notes. The trick to this method is to keep the information from the textbook and the notes together, and to separate chapters. With this format, a student is able to study the textbook and the lecture notes side-by-side, without wasting time or losing their train of thought by flipping back and forth between notes and textbook.

A variation of the split-page method is to divide the page into three columns. The middle column is used for taking notes in class. The left-hand column is used for outlining the text. The right-hand column is used for writing down keywords, cues, and questions the student may have about the material. This format provides the textbook and notes in one location, and has the bonus of a cue column. This allows students to cover the first two columns and use the cues in the third column as memory prompts when reciting the information.

SPLIT PAGE METHOD TEMPLATE

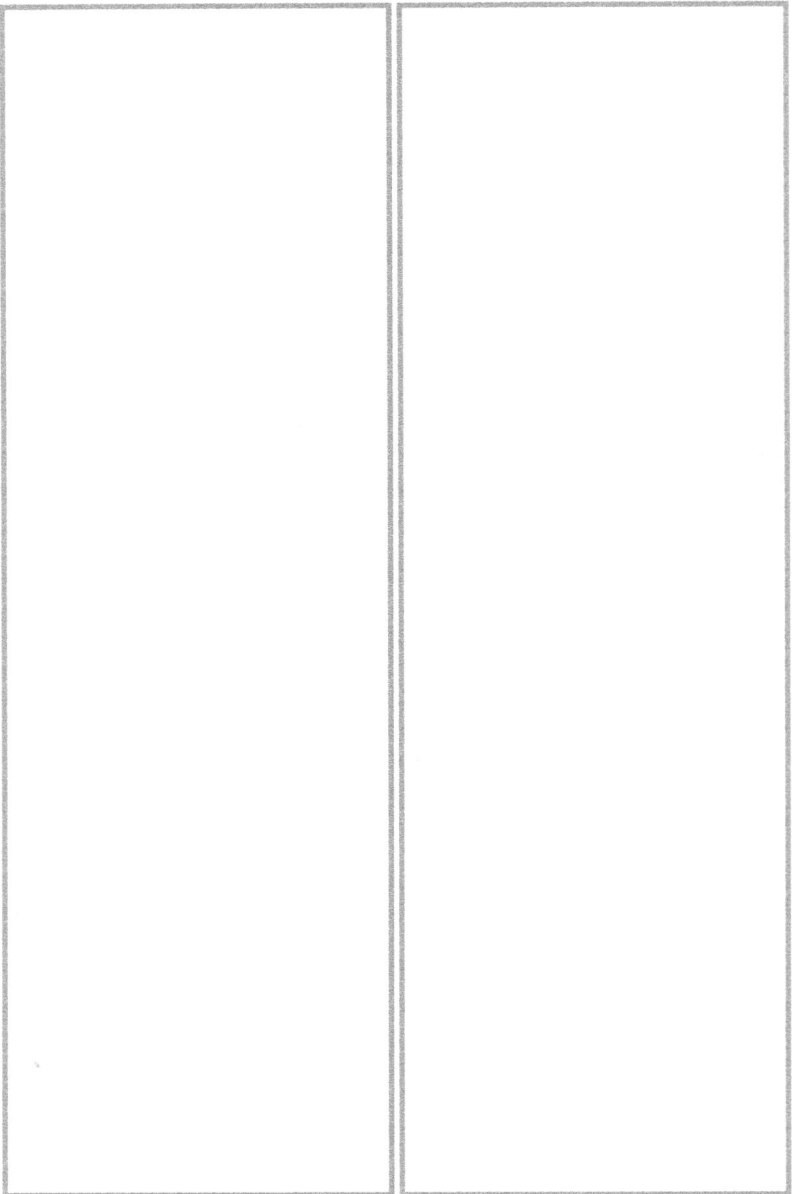

MIND MAPPING

Power
↑   Communism
| ↑
ANIMAL FARM
  /   Pigs
 /   ↓
Revolution   Humans

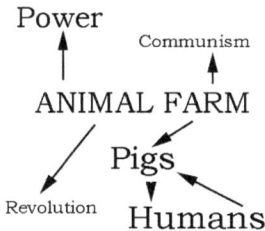

The traditional way to take notes is to write down the main concepts and sub topics as quickly as possible during a lecture and then make corrections later to fill in any gaps.

The problem with this process is it is linear and doesn't really involve any thinking – it is just a straight recording function, because time is short and generally doesn't record the interconnections between the concepts you have written down.

Mind mapping is a note taking technique where words, ideas, are linked to and arranged around a keyword or idea. Mind mapping allows you to generate, visualize, structure and classify ideas, quickly and easily.

Compared to other note taking methods, mind mapping generally takes less space and it claims to be a superior method in terms of learning and recall.

However, different methods work better for different people and often paying too much attention to the mechanics of note taking distracts from the content, which is after all the key.

The inventor and the trademark holder of the term "mind map" is Tony Buzan, who has created software that duplicates the brain's non-linear thought process.

Mapping & Mind Mapping

Mapping as a method of taking notes is similar to another concept, mind mapping. While mind mapping can be used as a note taking method it is also a way organizing information, brainstorming, planning and arranging information.

A mind map is a diagram used to represent words, ideas, tasks, or other items linked to and arranged around a central key word or idea. Mind maps are used to generate, visualize, structure, and classify ideas, and as an aid in study, organization, problem solving, decision making, and writing.

The mind map are arranged intuitively according to the importance of the concepts, and are classified into groupings, branches, or areas, with the goal of representing semantic or other connections between portions of information. Mind maps may also aid recall of existing memories.

By presenting ideas in a radial, graphical, non-linear manner, mind maps encourage a brainstorming approach to planning and organizational tasks. Though the branches of a mind map represent hierarchical tree structures, their radial arrangement disrupts the ranking of concepts typically associated with hierarchies presented with more linear visual cues. This orientation towards brainstorming encourages users to enumerate and connect concepts without a tendency to begin within a particular conceptual framework.

The mind map can be contrasted with the similar idea of concept mapping. The former is based on radial hierarchies and tree structures denoting relationships with a central governing concept, whereas concept maps are based on connections between concepts in more diverse patterns.

CHARTING METHOD

Charting is where you create a table with rows and columns to show information and the relationship between facts. Mapping is a picture of the ideas. The Outline method used one sentence on a separate line for each idea and the notes are like a table of contents or index.

NOTE TAKING PRACTICE

Below is a sample lecture or sample passage from a text book. The highlighted words in red are the important points in the passage, which form the basis of the notes.

Following this sample lecture, are sample notes in each of the 5 different methods explained above.

Read through the passage and as if you are reading a text-book or listening to a lecture, keeping in mind what you would write down as notes. Then go over the 5 different note taking styles examples.

SAMPLE PASSAGE 1

Clouds are divided into two categories, stratus clouds (or stratiform, the Latin stratus means layer) and cumulus clouds (or cumuliform; cumulus means piled up).
These two cloud types are divided into 4 more groups according to the cloud's altitude or height, High, Middle and Low.

High clouds
These generally form above 16,500 feet (5,000 m), in the troposphere. The prefix cirro- or cirrus is used on all high cloud names. At this height, water freezes so clouds are made of ice crystals. High clouds tend to be wispy, and are often see through.
High Clouds include Cirrus, Cirrostratus and Cirrocumulus.

Middle clouds
These clouds develop between 6,500 and 16,500 feet (between 2,000 and 5,000 m). The prefix alto- is used on all Middle clouds. These clouds are made of water droplets.
Middle Clouds include Altostratus and Altocumulus.

Low clouds
Low Clouds are found up to 6,500 feet (2,000 m) and include the stratus (dense and grey). When stratus clouds contact the ground, they are called fog.
Low Clouds include, Stratus, Nimbostratus and Stratocumulus.

SCAN FOR LECTURE

OUTLINE METHOD NOTES - PASSAGE 1

1. Clouds

    A. 2 categories stratus and cumulus. 3 more groups by height, High, Middle, and Low.

    A. High Clouds

        1. above 16,500 feet

        2. prefix cirro-

        3. made of ice

        4. wispy

        5. cirrus, cirrostratus, cirrocumulus

    C. Middle Clouds

        1. 6,600 – 16,500 ft.

        2. prefix alto-

        3. made of water drops

        4. altostratus, altocumulus

    D. Low Clouds

        1. up to 6,500 ft.

        2. stratus, nimbostratus, stratocumulus

SPLIT PAGE METHOD - PASSAGE 1

2 categories stratus and cumulus. 3 more groups by height, High, Middle, and Low. High Clouds above 16,500 ft prefix cirro- made of ice wispy cirrus, cirrostratus, cirrocumulus Middle Clouds 6,600 – 16,500 ft. prefix alto- made of water drops altostratus, altocumulus Low Clouds up to 6,500 ft. stratus, nimbostratus, stratocumulus	2 categories, stratus clouds cumulus clouds 4 groups High, Middle and Low. High These generally form above 16,500 feet (5,000 m), in the troposphere. The prefix cirro- or cirrus is used on all high cloud names. water freezes ice crystals. High clouds see through. Cirrus, Cirrostratus and Cirrocumulus. Middle 6,500 and 16,500 feet made of water droplets. Altostratus and Altocumulus. Low up to 6,500 fee t dense grey On Ground - fog. Stratus, Nimbostratus and Stratocumulus.

MIND MAP METHOD - PASSAGE 1

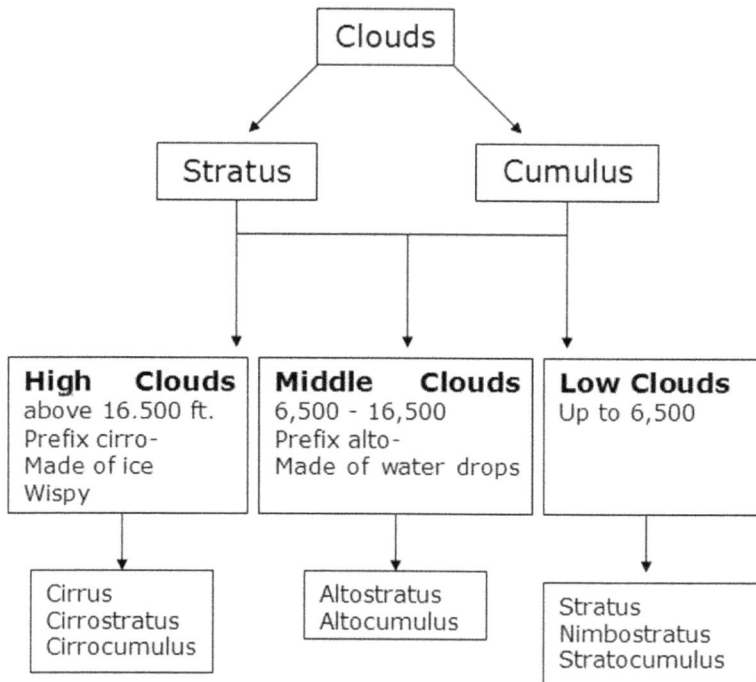

```
                        ┌──────────────┐
                        │   Clouds     │
                        └──────────────┘
                         ╱            ╲
              ┌──────────────┐   ┌──────────────┐
              │   Stratus    │   │   Cumulus    │
              └──────────────┘   └──────────────┘
```

High Clouds	**Middle Clouds**	**Low Clouds**
above 16.500 ft.	6,500 - 16,500	Up to 6,500
Prefix cirro-	Prefix alto-	
Made of ice	Made of water drops	
Wispy		

Cirrus	Altostratus	Stratus
Cirrostratus	Altocumulus	Nimbostratus
Cirrocumulus		Stratocumulus

CORNELL METHOD PASSAGE 1

2 categories stratus and cumulus. 3 more groups by height, High, Middle, and Low.	2 categories, stratus clouds cumulus clouds 4 groups High, Middle and Low.
High Clouds above 16,500 ft prefix cirro- made of ice wispy cirrus, cirrostratus, cirrocumulus	High These generally form above 16,500 feet (5,000 m), in the troposphere. The prefix cirro- or cirrus is used on all high cloud names. water freezes ice crystals. High clouds see through. Cirrus, Cirrostratus and Cirrocumulus.
Middle Clouds 6,600 – 16,500 ft. prefix alto- made of water drops altostratus, altocumulus	Middle 6,500 and 16,500 feet made of water droplets. Altostratus and Altocumulus.
Low Clouds up to 6,500 ft. stratus, nimbostratus, stratocumulus	Low up to 6,500 fee t dense grey On Ground - fog. Stratus, Nimbostratus and Stratocumulus.

3 types of clouds by height - High above 16,500 ft ,prefix cirro- made of ice wispy cirrus, cirrostratus, cirrocumulus. Middle 6,600 – 16,500 ft. alto- water drops, altostratus, altocumulus. Low up to 6,500 ft. stratus, nimbostratus, stratocumulus

CHARTING METHOD PASSAGE 1

2 Categories – Stratus and Cumulus 3 more groups, by height, High, Middle, Low

High	Middle	Low
Above 16,500 ft	6500- 16,500 ft.	Up to 6,500 ft.
Prefix cirro-	Prefix alto-	
Made of ice	Made of water drops	
Cirruc Cirrostratus Cirrocumulus	Altostratus Altocumulus	Stratus Nimbostratus Stratocumulus

SAMPLE PASSAGE 2 - PLANETS

A planet is a large round mass in orbit around a star.
The name comes from the Greek term planētēs, meaning
"wanderer", as ancient astronomers noted how lights moved
across the sky.

The International Astronomical Union lists nine planets in
our solar system. The planets in our system are Mercury,
Venus, Earth, Mars, Jupiter, Saturn, Uranus, Neptune, and
Pluto.

The word "planet" does not have a precise scientific definition, and so many astronomers argue that Pluto should be
removed from the list while others argue the number of planets should be raised to ten or even higher depending on how
planets are defined.

The International Astronomical Union, after much debate
recently decided Pluto is not a planet.

A large round object was found between Mars and Jupiter,
named Ceres, which was called a planet at first, but later
classified as an asteroid.

Many large round objects have been seen beyond Neptune,
including Sedna, but they have not been recognized as planets by the International Astronomical Union.

Scan for Lecture

OUTLINE METHOD - PASSAGE 2

1. Planet
   a. Comes From Greek word, Planetes, or wanderer.
   b. Large, round mass and orbits around a star.
   c. Nine planets in our solar system.

      Mercury
      Venus
      Earth
      Mars
      Jupiter
      Saturn
      Uranus
      Neptune

   d. No precise scientific definition.

2. International Astronomical Union
   a. Lists Planets in our solar system.
   b. Expected to define planets better
   c. Decided Pluto is not a planet

3. Non-Planets
   a. Ceres - Between Mars and Jupiter
   b. Sedna - Past Neptune

MIND MAP METHOD - PASSAGE 2

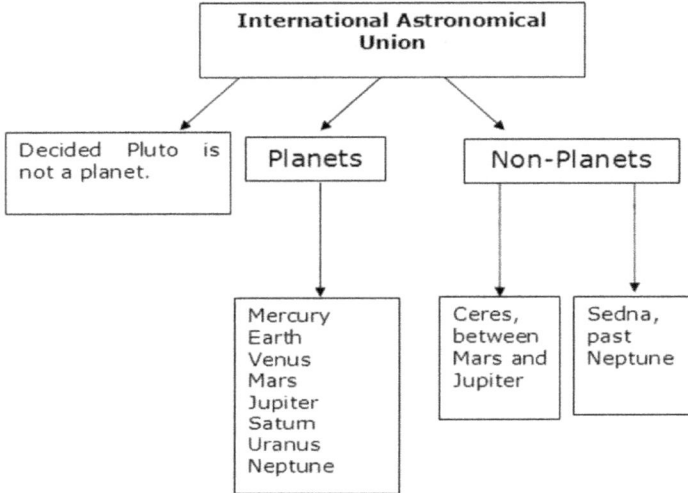

```
                    ┌──────────────────────────┐
                    │ International Astronomical│
                    │          Union            │
                    └──────────────────────────┘
         ┌───────────────┬──────────────┬───────────────┐
         ▼               ▼                              ▼
┌──────────────────┐  ┌─────────────┐        ┌────────────────┐
│ Decided  Pluto is│  │   Planets   │        │  Non-Planets   │
│ not a planet.    │  └─────────────┘        └────────────────┘
└──────────────────┘         │                       │
                             ▼                ┌───────┴────────┐
                    ┌─────────────┐           ▼                ▼
                    │ Mercury     │    ┌────────────┐  ┌────────────┐
                    │ Earth       │    │ Ceres,     │  │ Sedna,     │
                    │ Venus       │    │ between    │  │ past       │
                    │ Mars        │    │ Mars and   │  │ Neptune    │
                    │ Jupiter     │    │ Jupiter    │  └────────────┘
                    │ Satum       │    └────────────┘
                    │ Uranus      │
                    │ Neptune     │
                    └─────────────┘
```

CHARTING METHOD NOTES - PASSAGE 2

Planets: Large round mass that orbits around a star; 9 listed in our system, comes from Greek word "Planetes" meaning wanderer.

Planets	Non-Planets	Int. Astronomical Union
Mercury Earth Venus Mars Jupiter Saturn Uranus Neptune	Ceres, between Mars and Jupiter	Lists Planets In our Solar system
	Sedna, past Neptune	Decided Pluto is not a planet

CORNELL METHOD - PASSAGE 2

Planet- From Greek, Planetes, = wanderer	Planet - from Greek Planetes, or wanderer
	No precise scientific def.
No precise scientific definition	
	Lge, round mass orbits star
Large, round mass that orbits a star.	9 planets - Mercury, Venus, Earth, Mars,
9 planets in solar system - Mercury, Venus, Earth, Mars, Jupiter, Saturn, Uranus, Neptune	Jupiter, Saturn, Uranus, Neptune
	Int. Astronomical Union - decides
Int. Astronomical Union Will define planets better	IAU will define planets better
Decided - Pluto not a planet	IAU decided Pluto not planet
	Non-Planets in S. System
Non-Planets Ceres Between Mars & Jupiter	Ceres - Mars - Jupiter
Sedna - Past Neptune	Sedna - Past Neptune

9 planets in solar - Mercury, Venus, Earth, Mars, Jupiter, Saturn, Uranus, Neptune

Planet (Greek, Planetes, = wanderer) large round mass orbiting - no precise def. Int. Astronomical Union - decides - Will define planets better

IAU Decided - Pluto not a planet

Non-Planets in S. system - Ceres Between Mars & Jupiter & Sedna - Past Neptune

SPLIT PAGE METHOD - PASSAGE 2

Planet - from Greek Planetes, or wanderer No precise scientific def. Lge, round mass orbits star 9 planets - Mercury, Venus, Earth, Mars, Jupiter, Saturn, Uranus, Neptune Int. Astronomical Union - decides IAU will define planets better IAU decided Pluto not planet Non-Planets in S. System Ceres - Mars - Jupiter Sedna - Past Neptune	Planet - from Greek Planetes, or wanderer No precise scientific def. Lge, round mass orbits star 9 planets - Mercury, Venus, Earth, Mars, Jupiter, Saturn, Uranus, Neptune Int. Astronomical Union - decides IAU will define planets better IAU decided Pluto not planet Non-Planets in S. System Ceres - Mars - Jupiter Sedna - Past Neptune

STUDYING

How NOT to Study - the Complete Guide to Totally Failing

Don't Plan Your Time

Who needs to use an agenda to organize their time? Who needs it to list all their assignments? It's much easier to forget about all the assignments that pile up over the semester. When the due date comes, you can always shake your fists in frustration for being so disorganized.

Also, it's too hard to pack a tiny agenda into your backpack – it's not worth having an extra book to track your assignments.

[**In Reality** – you really need to get woke – Here is how to plan]

Don't Take Care of Your Physical Health.

Junk food at all hours of the day is more fun than a balanced diet. It'll prevent you from thinking clearly and maintaining a good sleep schedule, which is totally ideal, right? Snacking and studying

Eating a whole family-pack of chips for breakfast before an exam is filling, cheap, and gives you enough starch to last through the first part of the exam. If you pass out halfway through the exam, hey, that's okay! At least you had enough nutrition to last halfway.

DON'T PRIORITIZE YOUR MENTAL HEALTH.

Mental health? What's that? Must be a hippie, pseudo-science thing. It's not real! The only thing you care about is your grades, and who cares about mental health?
No need to vent stress every once in a while, – you can handle it without talking to your friends or family, who are supposedly there to support you.

[In Reality – Handle that – Mental Prep for a Test — Plan of Attack – Ready for Battle — Study without going Insane]

DON'T ASK FOR HELP.

You don't need to go to the professor's office hours – those are for people who are really dumb, right? And your grades can't be improved – you must be at the top of your class now! Your TA is also too intimidating to visit. You can probably get the best answers from your peers, not the people who set the actual exam questions.

[In Reality – Get Help]

DON'T JOIN CLUBS OR ASSOCIATIONS, AND DON'T TAKE EXTRA CURRICULARS SERIOUSLY.

Why bother trying something new or challenging? You're already busy with your regular coursework, and extra-curriculars will just add more stress to your schedule. You don't need to be well-balanced, and you don't need a social life nor networking. In fact, you don't think networking is needed to meet influential people in your field of study, right?

And sports! Who needs to run around, puffing and getting fit every week? You can gain the 'freshman 15' and keep it – who cares? It's too much work to exercise every once in a while.

GET OUT THE CELLPHONE!

Bring out your cellphone in class and Snapchat your buddy with the dullest photo you can think of. You may also decide

that Instagram is a better use of your life or take the time to catch some Z's. When the exam rolls around, you will have never seen the information and it will become some sort of gambling game. Maybe try all B's?
[**In reality** – NO!   The instructional period is the most important part of your studying. Take the time to learn it well and you won't forget it. Ask your teacher questions if you can't understand some of the material. Also, don't forget to take brief, HANDWRITTEN notes to help your brain absorb the information easier. No typed notes, folks. Research has proven that handwriting requires deeper cognitive processing causing you to understand it better. What about taking pictures of the teacher's notes? True scholars will enjoy note taking. Taking pictures is for those who are too lazy to care about school—most of them will never revisit the photo to glean its information.] How to take notes How to handle distraction

Hang Out

Hang out with friends every evening. Shove your notes and textbooks under the table to make room for your night-long game of Monopoly. If you are feeling especially adventurous, "forget" your material in your school locker—who needs it anyway?

[**In reality** – Revisit your notes several times leading up to the exam. Refresh yourself on the material every once in a while and make sure it is committed to your long-term memory. For most courses, I do not suggest studying by reading the textbook. There is a lot of distractor information (unrelated to what you need to know) that will get you off track. Your notes, either from a teacher or self-made, will be extremely beneficial in directing you to the important material you absolutely need to understand. Quizzes are extremely useful as well. They show you where your understanding is flawed and where to study further. As a junior high school teacher once taught me; study what you don't know, not what you know. You will also need to get a good amount of sleep every night. Sleep deprivation severely hinders your brain's ability to function leading to forgetfulness and napping during class.]

PULL AN ALL-NIGHTER! YEA!

Try to cram every bit of information you never learned into your brain. When fatigue begins to set in, drink a couple of red bulls and watch a funny cat video on YouTube to fight your boredom.

[**In Reality** – its fifty o'clock – it's too late to learn the information now. Anything you commit to memory will be short-term and likely forgotten after the test. Best thing to do here is briefly review your notes and get a good night's sleep.]

Sometimes life happens – if you really have to – here is the complete guide to cramming – How to Cram — How I swam without having to cram

IT'S TEST DAY!

You will still be awake cramming information. Skip breakfast to buy a bit more time. If you are late for school as well, even better! You will be so stressed out and tired that you won't even be able to think during the test.

[**In Reality** – Get some Shuteye. Sleep deprivation is dangerous during an exam. You may comprehend the test question in a way unthinkable to a well-rested brain ultimately leading to the wrong answer. Make sure you also eat a well-balanced breakfast with the nutrients you will need to keep your brain running through the test. If you still feel unsure of yourself, you may choose to do a quick review of your notes before the test—specifically committing a couple facts or values you may not have remembered otherwise to short-term memory.]

STUDYING

Sounds simple, right? But studying is a learned skill. It requires commitment, an understanding of the course expectations, time and materials. Most of all, successful studying takes practice. That means showing up everyday and viewing the act of studying as an integral part of student life.

Education is an investment in yourself. A healthy approach to any academic endeavor is to first realize that anything worth your time is worth doing to the best of your ability. Your academic success is directly proportional to the effort you put into your work. Nobody can do it for you. Like any large-scale project, it is important to have clear goals and a plan, which we talked about in Chapter 1.

Before you can create an effective study plan it is essential to understand what it is you are expected to learn. Some important things to think about are the amount of work required to prepare for an exam and the time frame you have to work in. What kind of test are you preparing for? A good place to start is with the course syllabus, which should outline the objectives of the class. Another valuable organizing tool is the table of contents of the course textbook. Think about and try to understand your instructor's teaching style. Some rely heavily on the text, or lecture or on-line supplements or any combination of source materials. The point is whatever materials your instructor places importance on should be viewed as valuable resources for your studying.

Once you know what you will be expected to know, you can begin to study actively. Successful learning is a long-term process, and it requires ongoing attention. Time is crucial to smart studying. Often finding a consistent schedule for study time is a key to success. As you plan your study schedule, consider that you will want to be fed, rested and sober to function at your highest academic potential. Dedicate time for each individual academic responsibility based on the amount of effort you need to stay on top of the workload. Then use that time for the subject at hand, resisting the urge to attend to other duties. Staying on task improves overall productivity.

Go from weak to strong. Areas of the material where you struggle need extra attention — study those areas first. The material where you are strongest will require less time and can be reviewed closer to test time.

CONCENTRATING ON WHAT MATTERS

When you know that tomorrow's test is a major part of your grade, the pressure can make it difficult to concentrate. You might spend hours with your nose in the book, but you are just not absorbing much. It feels like you are being pushed from all sides and there is so much commotion going on around you that you can't begin to concentrate. What to do? Where to begin?

Calm Down. Concentration requires a calm, well-organized place to study. Your home—be it a dorm room, an apartment or a house, might offer a private sanctuary where distractions will be at a minimum. Even a closet fitted with a desk might do the trick, but if you can't find the quiet you need to focus, look for a study area elsewhere. Whether it is the library, a friend's place or another quiet corner, it is essential to find a spot where the demands of the outside world recede.

Keep It Together. Do not leave for your study area without taking everything you might need, such as textbooks, computer, notebooks, CDs or anything else you might want at hand. If you have to break your concentration to fetch a pencil or a dictionary, it might be hard to get your focus back. Don't forget a snack and a drink to reward yourself and keep your energy up!

Rank and Pace Yourself. Knowing your strengths as well as your weaknesses will help you recognize what to focus on. Material you already understand, will not require much of your attention. What are your weak spots? What are the questions that might trip you up? Those are the ones to start with so you do not run out of time. Pacing yourself is important!

Take Five. Take breaks when your eyes get tired or you realize you have read the same passage a couple of times and didn't retain anything. Going on a short walk or making a cup of tea gives your mind a little time to clear. You will return to your studies feeling refreshed and ready to focus again. Remember that there is a limit to how much information your short term memory can store. Breaks are important because they allow new information time to process. When you take a test, you are pulling information from long term memory, which does a much better job of retaining it.

Things that interfere with Concentration:

- Clutter, noise, interruptions, phone, chat, people, etc.

- Common concentration issues:

- Your mind wanders from one thing to another

- Your worries distract you

- Outside distractions take you away before you know it

- The material is boring, difficult, and/or not interesting

Concentration Self Assessment

I can't concentrate because:

Too many distractions/interruptions

Describe: _____

_____

The material is boring and/or difficult

Don't have enough time

My mind wanders

Concentration Tips

- Turn off cell phone, TV, radio etc.

- Background music is ok as long as it doesn't distract.

- Put up a sign

- Set goals and reward yourself.

- Take frequent short breaks.

- Set a timer for 15, 20, 30, 45 minutes and work until the timer goes off then do something you like doing.

CONCENTRATION SOLUTIONS

Problem/Issue	Solution
Distractions/Interruptions	- improve study location - get a sign - turn off cell phone - collect all the material you will need (i.e. textbooks, notebook) BEFORE you begin.
Boring/Difficult	- Create rewards for successfully completing a task, such as calling a friend, a food treat, a walk, etc. -"If I study for 1 hour then I get a reward" - Changing the subject you study every one to two hours for variety - take regular breaks
Not Enough Time	- Schedule your time - Make a Weekly Schedule that includes studying
My mind wanders	- take regular breaks - before you begin set a goal (i.e. 30 minutes of study and then a break)

Student Tip - Try Over-Distracting Yourself

Just eliminate all distractions! Well, unfortunately it's not that easy for me. I will fiddle with my pen, doodle in the textbook, get lost in thought looking out the window, or make up a song while tapping on my desk. Thus, I have made myself the ultimate study strategy: over distract myself, the perpetually distracted.

Yes, you did indeed read that right. When I have only one thing in front of me that I don't want to do, my response is usually to find something else that can occupy my time. Whether it be my phone, my hair, or the loose rings on my fingers, I will, and I mean I WILL, find something else to do. Now, let's be clear here. I know I am not alone in this issue. I also know that most people suck it up and get the work done eventually, even though it is a struggle and a major grind to force yourself to pay attention to the task at hand. And yes, I could do the same. I could sit there and waste a bunch of my time like I did for many years. At least, up until I discovered this strategy that works way better than anyone could have ever guessed.

So this is where it may get a bit weird for people reading this with normal, functionable, and concentrated brains. In order to stop myself from getting distracted, I have to give myself distractions that will not hinder me, and yet will give me something to take my mind off how horrible I think studying is. The following is a true story about me studying for my physics exam last year. I set up my laptop in front of me and pulled up Disney plus. Once there, I opened up the movie 'The Emperor's New Groove" and watched it on repeat every time I studied. I know the movie so well that I did not actually need to pay attention to know what was going on, yet when the physics got to be too much for my brain to handle, rather than going on my phone or getting up for a boredom snack, I could snap back into my familiar movie bubble. The movie in the background was enough for me to be moderately entertained, while also not requiring my full attention. It helped me concentrate more on the task I had on hand and distracted me from thinking about and of my other distractions.

STUDENT TIP - GET LOTS GOING ON!

A major way that I learned how not to get distracted while studying was with having a background noise. Though this may not be a reasonable option for everyone but someone with ADHD, like myself, having multiple things going on at once truly helps a lot.

First thing that I did was go into my Spotify and create a playlist of songs that already loved and knew. By already knowing the words to the songs, it put my mind at ease. While if it were to be a new song that I did not know, I would try to focus on the lyrics and determine if liked it or not. Second, I noticed there were a lot of other playlist that were already created made for studying purposes and browsed through their music selection to see if there were any songs that I missed and added them to my own playlist.

STUDENT TIP - NO DISTRACTION! BOYCOTT THE INTERNET!

Phones have become one of the biggest distractions of our century. We use them for everything, but sometimes we might not know when to stop. If your phone distracts you, put it on airplane mode so that you won't hear that annoying ding sound that will destruct you from your studies. Another option is to turn it off completely or leave it in a different room from where you are studying. Always remember that your phone, social media and friends are always going to be there.

Studying is much more important to get you where you want to be and after you finish you will be able to go and browse the web all you want.

STUDENT TIP - DON'T BE AFRAID TO BLAST THE BEATS.

Now, one thing I've realized has kept me motivated for my study sessions are my music playlists. It might sound unconventional and like a bit of a distraction, I thought so too at first, but I urge you to try it at least once. Not only does it keep me extra focused on whatever task I have to accomplish, it keeps me alert and energetic. It drowns out the silence or anything that could possibly be a disturbance by being a consistent thing. I compile a playlist of songs of all genres that I'd enjoy but not songs that I know off-head (listening to an apple or Spotify playlist specifically for focusing helps too). I have a friend who listen to purely acoustics or drumbeats when studying. And Lately, I've been very inclined to Beethoven's symphony no. 5 in C minor. But regular pop, rock or indie beats work as well.

STUDENT TIP - ASSOCIATE WITH MUSIC!

Associating a melody to words allows our brains to remember them better. I have found that I am able to remember my notes much easier if I create a song about the topic I need to memorize. Whether you are a Grade 9 Royal Conservatory pianist, or just a person who taps their foot when a song is played in a coffee shop, you can use the foolproof method of syncing your study to music and greatly improve your academic achievement.

Here is the method I use: First, I write out all my notes and information that I need to memorize on a sheet of paper. These notes will become the lyrics to my song. Secondly, I pick a song that has been stuck in my head–one that I just can't seem to get out. These songs are the perfect melodies to use when I construct my study songs.

Next, I divide each section of the song (first verse, chorus, etc) into the different topics from my notes. After this, all I have to do is sing my notes to the tune of the catchy song I've chosen, singing about each topic during specific sections of the song. Then, I repeat! In the same way the radio plays certain songs over and over again, singing my study songs repeatedly–or even reciting them in my head–ensures that I remember all of my information on tests. Often, using this method hardly feels like studying; I am having fun, which motivates me to work more and relieves my stress, too.

STUDY TIP - MAKE TECHNOLOGY YOUR FRIEND

As the daughter of two teachers I've heard all the lectures about studying and let me tell you, I have done plenty of it! I'm finishing high school this year and my strategies of retaining information has given me confidence taking tests and feeling prepared. There are so many distractions with technology today so rather than allow it to be a hindrance I have practiced ways to use it toward my advantage.

First, collaborate and communicate with others. That is key to imbedding the information into your brain for recall. Form group chats on social media with classmates and ask questions and make comments. Forming a study group. This is powerful as you can read back over it and you look at the information while making connections. Substantiating information when your group chat members make comments allow you to understand the concepts on a more personal level. This increases the likelihood of remembering the information for recall on a test. To become test wise truly is a skill that anyone can learn; it becomes a matter of what works for various individuals. However, turning what could be a distraction into a method to aid you is a creative way to learn study material.

Your Personal Ted Talk
One of the most underrated tricks for remembering material is trying to explain that crap to someone else. Even if you THINK you understand something, trying to explain it to a friend or classmate can really put that understanding to the test. Grab your best friend, a fellow confused classmate, a family member or even a mirror, and do your best to explain whatever topic you need to know for that crazy history test. If you can successfully explain it to others, you not only gain confidence in your ability to comprehend said topic but a better understanding of the key components that make it up.

"Retweet" To A Real Human:
Second, if you think of the success of Twitter and the notion of people retweeting ideas to followers, I've come away with another strategy that has helped me achieve success with my studying. I take the material that I have come to understand through chatting and group discussions and repeat to a real human. To explain new concepts to someone who is neutral or has no background with what you're explaining can be advantageous as well. You therefore, become the teacher and the impact on overall cognition of facts is priceless! If you retweet or rather, 'repeat' to another person, you reach a deeper level of understanding within yourself.

Face The Book:
Finally, ditch your notifications on Facebook for a short time and face your book in solitude. Read over the information, make notes and comments on the margin or in a notebook. This final solidifying of facts and connections that you've made written out allow you to seal the deal, for the test. Tricks for memory like acronyms would be useful at this point as you make the notes for yourself. Similar to skimming over your notifications or newsfeed of your friend list, skimming over your notebook of thoughts and comments allows you to take in the information in the same way as Facebook.

Technology is part of our lives and we can't deny that it is an integral part of how we function every day. To expect us to study or learn new information while casting that integral part aside is rather ludicrous. I have come to utilize my social media and devices for my benefit toward studying and achieving good grades. Parking your cell phone aside has its place on occasion, but in many cases, it can indeed, be your greatest support if used the correct way. So get snapping, and achieve today!

STUDENT TIP AVOIDING THE TIK TOK RABBIT HOLE:

As a member of Gen Z, I admit, I am 100% addicted to tik tok. So far down the rabbit hole, at this point that I doubt anyone could save me. So getting off tik tok and forcing myself to study proves to be a slightly difficult task. What do I personally do, you may ask? I power off my phone and literally chuck it underneath my bed so that I physically can't go on it. But do what you need to do. If you need to lock your phone in a safe, do it. I'm not here to judge. I promise it'll help. Because trust me, what feels like five minutes on tik tok is actually an hour. And if you continue down that path, you'll end up accomplishing absolutely nothing. So just do it. Your friends and tik tok can wait.

STUDY GROUPS

Study groups are a great way to supplement your individual study. Being involved in a study group provides you with the opportunity to get feedback on how well you know the material, as well as reinforcing what you have learned. In addition, a good study group gives you practice at working as part of a team, a skill that you will need in the world outside school.

Explaining or teaching someone else is one best way to learn something. In a study group, others will be able to explain things to you and you will be able to explain things to them and you will both learn more than studying by yourself.

Here are some tips for forming a good study group:

- Talk to other students before and after class and during breaks. This will give you the chance to find out which students you can work well with, as well as which students know something about the material and work at succeeding in the class.

• Make sure you have enough group members that you still have a functioning group if one member can't make it, but keep the group small enough that you are able to accomplish goals during study sessions. A group of 5 or 6, including you, is usually a good size.

• If you are uncomfortable approaching other students, ask the professor or teacher if they can pass around a sign-up sheet.

• Set a meeting time that works for everyone's schedules.

• Schedule enough time to cover material thoroughly. Too many days throughout the week can be a bit daunting for some, and too little really gets you nowhere, so a good goal for any group is to meet three to four days a week. This allows the people in the group to go over materials on their own, and bring any questions that arise to the group at the next meeting.

• Choose a location that will be free of distractions and interruptions. Make sure the environment is comfortable because you will be spending a great deal of time there.

There are two ways to approach study group sessions, and you will need to take the approach that best suits your group.

Formal group – At the end of each study session, write an agenda for the next session. Assign topics or sections for each group member to present.

Informal group – At the beginning of each study session, decide which areas will be covered. You can cover those by having group members present different areas or through group discussion.

At some point, every study group will start to veer off track. The following tips will help get the group refocused and prevent it from becoming a social group:

• Set a schedule. Decide ahead of time when the study session will end. Schedule time for breaks, too. This makes it clear how much time is available to cover the material.

• Stay on Track. When students in the group begin venturing off track with their discussions, simply ask them if that material is on the test.

• Everyone comes prepared. Don't allow group members to come unprepared. Often, establishing preparation as a rule when forming the group will be enough.

• Stay on Topic. Remember that the study group meets to study the material. Complaints about professors, teachers and classes should be saved for scheduled breaks, or kept to a minimum.

A well-formed and focused study group can be a valuable tool for learning. The interaction and support from the group will help you stay motivated, and group feedback will help you discover your strong points and weak areas.

DISADVANTAGES OF STUDY GROUPS

Some disadvantages to studying in a group might be that some students tend to take over and focus on what they want to study or discuss rather than making it an interactive session with everyone participating. Some people might feel intimidated to speak up if they disagree and might not feel confident about interrupting others. Study groups can also deteriorate into discussions that go nowhere and accomplish nothing about learning with some becoming more of a social networking group rather than serious study.

It probably depends on the student to determine whether the benefits outweigh the negatives. It might be helpful to use a study group as a resource to aid in research of a particular topic but not to use this avenue as a regular course of action when studying for an exam – particularly a meaningful one. In other words, use a study group as one way to study for a particular topic – but routinely use other methods that rely on your own instincts rather than those of others.

How to Study from your Notes

Using your class lecture notes may not be as intuitive as reading the textbook, but once you learn how to study from your lecture notes, you'll learn more quickly.

A key reason students fail to use and study from their classroom notes is they believe the notes to be incomplete. If you feel you are missing key information in your class notes, join a study group and help each other fill in the missing blanks.

You may find it easier to take notes on your computer or type them out neatly after class.

Whatever note taking method you determine is ideal for you, use paper notes when it is time to study. Collect your notes and use them to clarify the information you are reading and studying.

Incorporating your class notes into your study sessions can help you to learn more information in a quicker manner. Reading your textbook will be easier if you use your class lecture notes to guide your reading and refresh your memory during the first part of your study session. Your classroom notes can be a helpful tool to your entire learning process. Use them.

Rewriting your Notes

One of the best way to study to rewrite and summarize your notes at home. Reading them over has value, but actively rewriting (or, to a lesser degree, typing) them has extra value because it helps you memorize them .

Rewriting your notes accomplishes several goals:

It makes them neat, legible and better organized for future studying. You might decide to convert them to one of the note taking methods discussed in Chapter 4. Some students like to convert them into a mind map, which can be a more efficient way of sorting and absorbing the material.

You have to think about everything you're copying, which helps to replay the class in your mind and sink the material deeper into your memory.

You can consult your texts and fill in any missing information, so you have complete notes in one place when it comes time to study for exams.

1. **When you actively write the words again, you are studying them**. If you are a kinesthetic learner (Chapter 1), you'll be doing yourself a huge favor because the physical act of writing things down a second time deeply reinforces it in your memory.

2. **You might discover something you didn't understand.** Take the time to write down the question and ask your instructor or take it to your study group.

3. **When it comes time to review for exams, you don't have to cram** because you've been actively studying all through the term.

Remember that your notes are for you. They don't have to follow any exact method, as long as they work for you.

How to Study Text Books

The reading of textbooks is an integral and unavoidable part of your college education. Although in the classroom a teacher may cover much of the content of the subject matter, many of the details of the topic will be fleshed out from your textbook. Unfortunately much of the material you will encounter in a textbook can be dry, making it difficult to stay focused and study. Concentration is essential to your success in the class.

All of the material you are required to learn is crucial for your success. Especially at a collegiate level, professors don't just assign busy work, so everything you read has a meaning. The readings in a textbook will show up throughout the course in homework, class discussions, tests, and projects, so it is up to you to have a thorough understanding to contribute to the conversation. At this upper level of education, some of the readings can be dense and difficult to understand, which is why you need to create methods and study skills to tackle these texts in an efficient manner.

A Systematic Method for Studying Textbooks

To glean the essential information needed from your textbook it is important to follow a systematic process. This will help you retain more of what you read and build a solid base of knowledge, which in turn will make it easier to study for the next test. We've provided you with a process along with other methods, for you to maximize your studying time and thoroughly learn the material.

Review The Title And Headers Of The Chapter You Are Reading

If you are following instructions to build something, you will most likely review all of the instructions first before physically beginning. This preview allows you to get a sense of what you will encounter and how that material will progress through the textbook.

This act is called Surveying. Surveying gives you an overview of what you are about to delve into and lets you familiarize yourself with the main concepts. With this action, you can prepare an outline or flow of the materials you are about to cover in your reading. It allows your mind to organize and prepare for the subject matter. In addition to the titles, also read the graphs, pictures, etc. to immerse yourself in the text.

Convert the Chapter Headings or Main Ideas into Questions.

Ask yourself who, what, when, where, why or how. Write these questions down. This allows you to focus in on what you are reading and gives you purpose, so that you are not aimlessly reading. Once you've read through a section, highlight of a couple pieces that sums up the main ideas or seem important. Don't overdo the highlighting, as you should be able to read the key parts quickly without going over the whole paragraph. Use your notes or the margins of the text to write in questions that could be answered by the high-lighted information.

As tempting as it may be, don't take notes or highlight while you are reading through the text for the first time. This action can not only distract you from the material, but unless you've read the whole text, you won't know which parts are important enough to highlight.

Note any Additional Subheadings with Questions.
After you've finished reading the chapter, go back to your paper and make sure all of your written questions have been answered in a complete manner. Make sure there are no other questions that come to mind that need answering.

As important as it is to have a full understanding of the material, you should keep your responses to the questions concise. Otherwise, you might as well be reading the exact text.

Don't forget to pay attention to any tables, charts, and pho-tographs that are mentioned in the textbook. There is often additional information set aside in boxes on the pages that add to what is written in the body of the text. Take care to note or highlight this information as well as they are usually important.

Finally, Review the Chapter Summary and Complete the Questions at the end of the Chapter.

Use your notes to complete the answers, and write down any questions you didn't find in your own notes. As you go back through the chapter underline the proper heading to locate these unanswered questions and write them on your paper along with the question.

Ultimately, after finishing the reading you should be able to answer the questions you wrote down. If you do happen to struggle with them, then you can just check the highlighted portions. Keeping a written question and answer format of your textbook reading will help you when you are involved in classroom discussion. It will allow you to probe your teacher for any answers that weren't clear to you during the reading, and will make studying for your test that much easier.

You should also write other questions or observations, so you can bring these questions up during class or to your professor, which will give you a deeper understanding of the material. Especially in college, most professors have in-depth class discussions about the textbook readings. These discussions tend to count as a grade for class participation, so you want to make sure you are prepared and able to add your own opinion into the conversation.
Survey on how to study textbooks

Other Details while Studying a Textbook

The information in a textbook will be easier to understand when you put it into your own words. This translation simplifies the text into terms that you are familiar with, so you can easily explain the information or answer questions. It improves your comprehension of the material and not just the memorization. Keeping it in your own words is also helpful for when you need to write essays as it prevents the likelihood of plagiarizing.

Be creative when writing the questions and answers, so that you are engaged while studying. Create note cards or a study guide along with the text that you will understand and enjoy completing. Or come with up quizzes and games that you can exchange with a peer.

Increase your learning pathways. Instead of just reading the text try visualizing, listening, or using a hands-on approach to learning. Simply reading and writing isn't an effective learning method for everyone.

Work with a partner. After you've done the reading and taken notes, try working with a peer to review the information. They could help you with difficult parts and quiz you to ensure comprehension. Also, if you are teaching or discussing the material with them, then you have a higher chance of being able to recall that information yourself.

Read out loud. Hearing the words as you read with a physical voice—not just the one in your head—processes in your
brain differently and increases your ability to remember.
Use the keys in a textbook, the internet, or a dictionary
to define any words or references that you do not know or
struggle with to avoid confusion.

If you are have trouble understanding the material, then
seek help from your teacher, a tutor, or even a friend. Another fresh perspective can explain the concepts to you in a
way you've never thought of before.

How do you study textbooks? A Quick Survey

Best way to Study Textbooks?

Here is the method that I used successfully. Whenever I
have a textbook to study, I first divide it into four main sections. After reading each section I make notes in a book not
the textbook, using my own words of the most important
points. I also make notes and marks in the textbook. When
I want review I review my own hand written notes, because
it is smaller in size and direct to the point. This system has
always helped me out.

You may Decide to Divide your Textbook into Five or Six Sections.

The aim is to make the textbook seem smaller as you attack
the sections one after the other. I also recommend that your
always study in a quiet environment. I prefer some low soft
music playing in the background when I study, but you need
to find out what works for you. Classical music stimulates
the mind.

I was a Very Good Student. Had Great Grades and was Brilliant at Science Subjects. Here are my Suggestions.

First thing I do is to skim through the textbook in a relaxed manner. I go through the chapters, headings, diagrams and pictures. The next day or two, I go through again, but this time I think and form opinions about what am reading. I then take down notes in my own words, highlighting the important points that would be helpful in a test.

I make sure I find answers to practice questions in the textbook, then practice drawing the diagrams and tables to get familiar with them. When I make revisions just before a test, I make use of my own handwritten notes.

I Would say it is Important you Start Making Notes as you Read.

Break up the textbook into smaller parts as that would help you concentrate better.

I also would suggest that you get a friend to hold the textbook and as you quiz questions to see how much you remember. Also read aloud as that helps a lot of students, and don't forget the practice questions in the textbook.

My own Method Involved First Writing an Outline for the Textbook Chapter I Want to Study.

This makes it easier to process all the dry data in textbooks. It also keeps you focused and expectant of the material. Next you take notes of the important points, focusing on understanding the main points and writing them down in your own words. This is a great way to instill what you read in your memory. When you are done, you have a great self-composed review note to read before the exam.

A lot of Students get Bored Reading Textbooks, it is not New and You are not Alone.

It happens to me often when am reading books on literature, history or grammar. It never happens when am studying my favorite subjects like math or biology.

So, I would advise you rest well before you study those boring subjects to keep you in an alert frame of mind. Study in a relaxed environment that would allow you concentrate. Study for short periods with breaks instead of a long extended period. Take down notes in your words and try reading out the material aloud.

As You Read, Make Notes of Important Stuff.

Before you proceed after a page or a heading, review to be sure you understood all the main points. Once you have, take a short break and resume after a few minutes. Always review all your notes at the end of each study session.

Go to the next section and repeat the whole process.

I Begin by Reading the Very First Paragraph of the Chapter.

Then I read the very first sentence of each subsequent paragraph, before reading the last paragraph of the chapter. This way I get an overview of the entire material I am about to read. It keeps my mind prepared and expectant, ready to absorb information. This process is called skimming and it helps you better understand and retain information.

Well it Depends on Your Age, Level and the Material Being Studied.

I would suggest regular breaks. Attention span is different for different people. Younger people tend to have shorter attention spans. So, if you are 15, take breaks after every 15 minutes of study. If you are older, you could study for longer periods. Making a study plan.

Some Tips for Studying Science Textbooks.

First look for books that teach you the basic rudiments.

For example, I used books like "A Short Course in General

Relativity" and Ryder's "An Introduction to Quantum Field Theory" to get basic ideas on GR and QFT. These books are not great or the best in the subject but they did provide me with the foundation basics in a simple to understand format. My point is, if you are having problem studying a textbook. Start from the lowest rung on the ladder and work your way up. Look for easier books that give basic information and then progress to the harder stuffs.

It Depends on the Type of Book and How Easy or Hard You Find the Subject.

For me, when reading a cool easy to read book I end up skimming through.

I would advise you to first skim through the book as if you were doing some leisure reading. This way you get familiar with what the book is about and some of the terminology used. After completing a section or chapter, I start all over but this time going through the textbook slower. I highlight key words or concepts in different colors. I also like to jot along margins and on the pages of the book. Finally I make my own notes by hand stating just the main points.

I would also advise that you do not restrict yourself to just one textbook for a subject. You would expand your knowledge when you read up various materials on the subject matter. Different authors have different ways and angles of presenting the same information.

Worst Way to Study Textbooks

Skim through an assigned chapter after lecture. Go through the assignments. The go back to the chapter, searching for similar problems or points to help you handle the assignments. Try to solve the assignment from information skimmed off the chapter. If you still cannot solve the assignment, go over the chapter again desperately looking for clues. It is either you do get clues to help you complete the assignment or your give up in frustration. Do the same thing next week and end up concluding the course is too difficult.

Proper Way to Study Textbooks

Read the chapter carefully and try to understand the material. Put down main points using your own words. Read aloud or look for ways to express what you have learned before an audience or study group. This would help you better understand the material and retain the information learned.

It is Important to Always Remember that Some Subjects Require That You Read and Study Actively, While Others may not.

For example, physics or math textbooks would require that you actively participate in solving questions, calculating and drawing tables and graphs.

This means that the best way to study such textbooks is to get involved in practicing the calculations, learning formulas, and drawing graphs from the very beginning. This way it becomes an integral part of you. If you read books without actively participating by making notes in your own words or highlighting key points, you would find it hard to remember what you read.

The First Step is to Determine Your Most Effective Learning Style.

Then gather learning resources to suit that style. Then go through the study material critically. Ask yourself questions along the way. Do you understand the concepts used? Do you see how the parts fit together? Will you be able to differentiate an idea based on facts or an idea based on data? Does what you read sound reasonable or believable?

This style of questioning what you read ensures you absorb the material fully. Make notes along the way and review your notes before exams.

Get a Notebook and Some Writing Material.

Gather several textbooks on one topic. Read the various

textbooks to get different angles to the material. Solve and practice any attached problems.

Make notes in your own words of the main points.

I Prefer Reading Slow.
This allows me to be meticulous when reading and not just to skim over pages. I try to get the sense of every paragraph before moving on. When studying equations and derivations I take even more time. I make notes of important points right inside the textbook. This helps me concentrate on the important points when I reread the material again. After completing a chapter or section and fully comprehending what it is all about, I revisit it again. This time I make my own notes in my own words highlighting the main points.

How to Study for a Math Test

Every subject has its own particular study method. Math is mostly numerical, not verbal and requires logical thinking; it has its own way to be studied. Before touching on significant points of studying a math test, lets look at some of the fundamentals of "learning."

Learning is not an instant experience; it is a procedure. Learning is a process not an event. Rome wasn't built in a day, and learning anything (or everything) isn't going to happen in a day either. You cannot expect to learn everything in one day, at night, before the test. It is important and necessary to learn day-by-day. Good time management plays a considerable role in learning. When you manage your time, and begin test preparation well in advance, you will notice the subjects are easier than you thought, or feared, and you will take the test without the stress of a sleepless body and an anxious mind.

Memorizing is a temporary step of learning if information is not comprehended and applied afterwards. Memorize just the basics and understand the meaning; then apply, analyze, synthesize and evaluate.

These are the hierarchical layout of cognitive learning: Of course, there are some basic properties that you need to memorize in the beginning, since you cannot prove the facts every time you solve a math test. For example; the inner angles of a triangle sum up to 180°. If you do not know this, you may not be able to solve triangle problems. And, more importantly, if you do not practice, you will certainly forget this property. Practice helps information take root in your brain.

Applying the same property on various types of questions extends the roots.

For example, if you see a triangle, you can analyze the question by means of the property. In a question, if you see a hexagon, you can split it into triangles and use the property, called synthesizing followed by evaluation. If all these steps are followed, the property is completely learned and has its place in your long term memory.

A useful method in providing consistent learning is using similarities between the information and events, images, shapes, … etc. For example, assume that you have difficulty remembering the formula $xa/yb = xay\text{-}b = 1/x\text{-}ayb$ in mind. You can associate this to an elevator: The exponents changing location (nominator/denominator) need to change exponent sign, similarly, people going up need to push the up button and if they decide to go down, they need to push the down button; so they need to change the button. Also; writing the formula in large letters and sticking it on a surface that is frequently visible helps memorizing it by using visual intelligence. The more senses (visual, musical, auditory, logical, …) the material addresses to, the more permanent it is.

Attend to all classes. Knowledge is not replaceable by others, and every brain is unique. You cannot learn math from your classmate's notes; take your own notes in your own understanding of the material. What you understand, or don't understand, and how you understand it is different to everyone else. Highlight the important points in your own way. Remember math and all other courses are mostly learned at school -practice comes afterwards at home.

Find your own way of learning. Every person learns and studies differently. Some take notes, some do not like writing; listening is the major way of embracing information for them, and some watch. It is important to detect the way that is more useful for you. Coloring important points also helps. Due to selective perception; we see the attractive words, signs before the rest. While studying math, make a list; first, determine the subjects you feel inadequate on and focus on them initially.

Never gloss over something that you do not fully understand. Information is built on previous learning in a hierarchical order. If you have question marks about a mathematical property, and don't understand is completely, you cannot solve problems using that property. You need to have a strong background to succeed in math.

You need to know your basic math inside out to do algebra. And you need to know your algebra inside out to do calculus. If you do not know exponentials, you cannot solve logarithms. If you don't understand something, get help from your teachers, reread course materials, resolve examples, discuss with friends or hire a private tutor.

Never skip over something that you don't understand – it will come back to haunt you!

Practice makes perfect! Yes – it really does! Working through math problems in your own way is essential. Looking over examples is a good first step – but only that. The example solutions shown in the textbook show you have to solve a problem, next you have to do it yourself. Do not miss to do your assignments. You see different types of examples and acquire different outlooks when facing math problems. Math is fun because usually there are many ways to reach the solution. Find alternative ways to solve a problem which anchors the learning deeper. Find similar and different problems, discuss with friends, ask each other questions. Observing other people's way of thinking, and solving problems will help both of you improves your minds.

Succeeding in math is a mental action. However, do not disregard physical and psychological effects. Always think positive and never give up; no success is gained without effort. Of course you will waste time solving problems which you will find easy, and you will struggle with difficult problems. In the end, you will be one step further ahead. And after more time spent practicing, you will be another step ahead.

Reward yourself after intense studies. This will keep your motivation high. The reward may be a chocolate bar, playing a game for 20 minutes, or taking a walk in the park. It is very essential to have a good night's sleep before taking a math test. Eating habits directly effect success. Keep away from fast food as much as you can, eat a light meal before a test. At last but not least, keep your inner motivation very high. Believe in yourself; you will certainly get the good result of your planned, efficient studies.

How to Study Science

Scientific Method is the Heart and Foundation of Studying Science

You may find some of the techniques and methods outlined here to be intimidating, and you may want to avoid them completely. Try them out and see which techniques suit your learning and studying style. All of them are designed to make it easy for you to make deep impressions of what you are reading, and then make useful associations that will help you remember the information when needed. All of them work but they don't all work for everyone. Any new technique is difficult at first and will improve with practice.

When Science is Difficult

Remind yourself that the difficulty in science is based on the nature of the subject.

Purpose: This will help you avoid giving up because you feel like a failure, or like it's your fault. Science courses contain new and difficult concepts and material, plus a great deal of problem-solving. This requires a different approach to studying.

Understand the Principles and Facts Before Memorizing Them

Purpose: Understanding the material will make it easier to memorize. As you study the material, you are unconsciously building your memory of the material.

Associate New Information With old Information

Purpose: Associations are important for memory. Associating new information to what you know is more effective than associating new information to other new material.

NEW -> OLD is better than NEW -> NEW

Make a habit of regularly asking "why or how does this new information make sense?" This helps to associate new material with what is already known.

Make Associations

Think about visual connections like a spider's web. Spiders don't create their webs by rushing through it, just like how you can't always rush through your study time or cram for a test the night before. Spiders start with a single thread and as they weave more, they slowly add more connections, improving the overall strength of their web.

Hopefully, this is what will happen by adding visual pathways to your studies. Adding these cues is like adding additional threads to your web of knowledge. As you add more you can improve your overall knowledge of your study material. Visual connections will help you to imagine an idea in multiple ways whether that be through written notes, your own comments or imagery that you've added.

Imagine this: You're studying chemical bonds between atoms and molecules. You're asked a question on the difference between substitutional and interstitial alloys in metallic bonding but you don't know how to explain it. If the only way you learned the difference between the two was memorizing the definition in your notes but you can't remember it in the moment, that's it; You can't answer the question. But if you were to use different kinds of visual connections, you might be able to answer the question even if you forget the exact definition. For example, when thinking about the answer, you remember the picture that you drew in your notes: a drawing of a series of circles of similar size to represent substitutional alloys and a collection of circles with smaller dots scattered in between the circles to represent interstitial alloys. It doesn't even have to be a drawing. You could have remembered that substitutional alloys looked like a game of connect four while interstitial alloys look more like Battleship with game pieces of different sizes. By using that imagery or visualization, you could infer that substitutional alloys are atoms of similar size beside each other while interstitial alloys have smaller atoms in between metal atoms. Visualization like this can help you understand and explain concepts without needing to strictly memorize an exact difference.

First Reading

Purpose of your first reading should be to understand what you read

Avoid using SQ3R or any other study systems the first time you read. Do not also try to memorize what you are reading.

Reason: When you read a science book you would be confronted with a big mass of complex and new material. Your mind has a big task trying to comprehend new ideas and concepts and breaking them down to simpler, easier to understand concepts. The survey in the first step helps with this. On the first reading, spend time to studying much more carefully, and attend classes that discussed it, and review your notes from those classes. Your mind will understand the material better, and the bigger relationships between the different sections of the material. Using SQ3R the very first time you read would make comprehension difficult. It would overload your working memory with large bits of information making you lose both your ability to understand and memorize the information.

Monitor your level of comprehension

Take note of meanings to check if you actually understand them or not. If you find a bit of information hard to understand, make use of study techniques to help you better comprehend.

Pause after natural units

Read, pause, then read and pause between paragraphs and short passages.

Purpose: Pausing while you read helps your mind organize and process the different parts of information so that you understand the entire unit. This assembling or organizing of meanings takes place automatically.

If come across cause and effects statements, descriptions or definitions you can use a simple style of marking. You can write D in the margin to denote a definition, F to indicate a descriptive face, and other simple alphabetical codes of your choice.

Mark any passage that seems difficult or you don't understand, so you can come back.

Purpose: To help you locate it later so as to reread it for better comprehension. The mark also prevents you from forgetting areas you were not clear on.

If you are having problems with a technical term, you can write it down along with its meaning and keep it close. You can also make a list of technical terms with their meanings and go over it regularly.

Review if necessary

If you read a chapter after taking a break from it, and then find it hard to understand because you no longer remember some of the things earlier read, you need to do a review. Reviewing what have been read before would make you remember key principles and concepts that will help you understand the rest of the chapter.

Associate what you are reading with mental images of the concrete events and things. Form visual images, imagined feelings of the movement and texture of events and objects. If the science material is abstract, form mental images of one or two specific things.

Read aloud in a normal conversational tone to yourself. If your location or situation does not allow you to read aloud, you can imagine yourself reading aloud and the sound of your voice. Translating printed or written text into words helps activate meanings.

Look repeatedly at text and related graphics to form a link between the text and the graphics related to it. When you look at the words and the graphics try to find out what each is trying to say and then see how they both are saying the same things.

When text or words are related to graphics, it makes them easier to understand and recall. Types of graphics would include diagrams, charts, graphs, pictures, and tables.

When you come across an analogy, you need to link the analogy to relevant technical descriptions, explanation and concepts. Analogies are very useful. Learn how to translate analogies, part by part to the related parallel parts of the material.

Use self-explanations to express the meaning of the material. Taking it section by section, translate meanings of what you read, form associations and then relate them to other parts of the material. Get interferences and try to match your mental model of the material match with the writer's.

Indicate paragraphs or passages not fully understood using a question mark. Remember to return to these sections when your mind is rested.

Classify Lectures And Texts Using Science Goals

The goals of science are to discover natural occurring phenomena, to explain, describe, predict and use natural phenomena. Science goals also seeks to support claims with evidence and sound reasoning.

When studying science you will see statements that describe, cause-and-effect statements to predict, explain or inform natural phenomena. You will also see definitions, concepts and arguments to support scientific claims, or prove that predictions, explanations and descriptions are valid.

As you study, try to classify the information into, cause and effect statements, descriptions, and reasoning or concept definitions.

Purpose: Helps identify what is important. Also helps organize the information into science patterns. Makes it easier to form associations to the information that would otherwise be difficult to form associations with.

Link Graphics and Text Together

Graphics and texts under the same topic should be translated into each other so that you can form a link between them. This means that when you see the text, you should be able to visualize the diagram, chart, picture or graph that displays the text.

Purpose: Helps to form associations in the mind that can link visual and verbal memories.

How to Handle Material That is not-too Meaningful and Without any Self-Association

An effective method is to try memorizing the material with common memorization methods. Psychologists listed the following as things that are relatively more difficult to learn: technical terms, proper names, formulas, dates, foreign words, formulas, arbitrary facts, and numbers. Information presented as a list may also be difficult to memorize. You can use memory techniques like frequent review, self-tests, and mnemonics.

Purpose: Building memory for material that may be hard-to-memorize.

Learning Skills—Reasoning Scientifically and Solving Problems

To build skills, avoid studying only the principles and knowledge while avoiding the problem solving questions. Go through already worked out problems, then practice and keep practicing for several days.

Purpose: To adapt study methods to different material and skills.

Use common good study methods faithfully in science

Purpose: helps ensure that you form accurate and effective learning skills within a relatively short time.

Survey The Material Before Reading

Surveying your reading material or chapter of a textbook be-fore reading, increases capacity to understand and retain new information. When you first survey new material, the patterns and information form a structure for associations, which builds memory. The more time you spend with the material the better acquainted with you become and the more it sticks to your memory.

A quick survey should be your first contact with the material. Diving straight into dense material gives the mind fewer op-portunities to make associations, and the text is confusing.

How to Survey

Spend about ten minutes figuring out what the chapter or textbook section contains. Skim through the introduction, vocabulary list, headings, main graphics, boldfaced material, any type of emphasized material, summary and even some of the self-test problems,

What to look for when doing a survey

Try to identify the information in the chapter that highlights the science goals such as the natural occurring phenomena discussed, cause and effects statements, descriptive state-ments, as well as the concepts and definitions. Also check if you can find scientific arguments that link theories to evi-dence, and if the chapter teachers specific problem solving skills.

What Should you Understand From A Survey?

Survey involves skimming through the material to form an idea on what it is about. Do not expect to fully comprehend the headings, vocabulary lists or summary of the chapter. Try to get a general overview of the information, even if you don't understand it fully. That is expected so do not worry. The aim is just to get a general idea and notice patterns to make the actual reading, in the next step, more productive.

If you study a section or chapter in more than one study session, you may have forgotten some of the information. Do a review of what you have read and survey again.

Purpose: To recall the main information and topics, which makes it easier to associate new information. Ensures that you do not read without forming associations.

Second Reading

The purpose of a second reading of the science material to identify statements that tally with science goals.

Purpose: To conduct a deep assessment or the material with the aim of understanding the material and to form associations that will build memory. As you read through the material, keep asking yourself the point being discussed in the sentence, phrases and paragraphs.

Read deep

Purpose: Read for a deeper understanding to build associations and improve memory. The second reading will be slow and hard work.

Take note of descriptions, definitions and cause and effect statements.

Mark cause and effect statements, descriptions and definitions and any other important concepts.

Next, identify the related parts of concepts and definitions

The definition of a concept includes the concept itself, the visual image, verbal definition, ways to measure the concept, and methods the concepts can be put to use to solve problems. (Measurement is vital because it is used by scientists to make explanations and descriptions precise and useful in gathering evidence.

Purpose: To bring all related parts of a concept together. Also helps prepare you to tackle test questions that link together examples, definitions and related procedures.

If you find several parts of a concept spread over the chapter, in several pages, note page numbers of related references close to the original concept definition.

Third, Identify Linked Theories and Evidence

Science textbooks often present a theory and then provide some evidence and research studies that bear both positively and negatively on the theory. Identify and mark the theory with the linked evidence. For example, a theory may be presented in page 55, while the evidence and studies are presented in pages 56, 57, 60 and 61. Here, indicate in the margin by the theory on page 55 "see pp. 56, 57, 60, 61." This will help later when doing your review. You would also be better prepared to answer test questions that request that involve both the theory and evidence.

Final Study Session

Focus on building memory for specific large blocks of information. At this stage focus on building memory for large chucks of information, especially information that is hard to understand. You need to make strong associations and impressions, to really 'own' the material and this will involve more time with the material.

MEMORIZING

If you are going to master the art of studying, you are going to have to master one of life's basic skills: memorization. Do not panic! It is not as hard as you might think. Learning a few basic memorization techniques will give you the skills you need to make learning and retaining information a cinch.

Repeat, Repeat, Repeat. Repetition is a clever way of convincing your brain that the material you are studying is important. That's because when an idea, a person, or an event is important to you, your mind will return to it again and again. By constantly and consistently reviewing new material, you will lock in the facts that you need to remember. Put simply, repetition saturates your brain with facts, words, and ideas to the point that you can't help but to remember them later on when you need them for a test.

Write It Down. Writing notes in class is really just a way of repeating information. In fact, that is one of the best reasons to take notes when you are in class and then rewrite them at home. When the professor says something and you write it down, that is one repetition. At home, when you review your notes, that is a second repetition. Re-writing the notes gives you a third opportunity to lock in the details. Any time you write something down, you're more likely to remember better than if you just read it. Getting your body involved in the learning process is kinetic. The words become etched, not just on your paper, but in your mind as well, because you associate the words themselves with the physical memory of having written them down in the first place.

When you combine writing with repetition, your brain recognizes the importance of the material you are asking it absorb and stores it where you will be able to access it quickly and easily when you need to. Individuals who have grown up with computers might find that taking notes on a keyboard helps them lock the information in more deeply. Older students, who grew up with paper and pens, might find the kinetic connection between mind and body works best when taking notes the old fashioned way. Writing notes by hand further locks in the material simply because it takes longer. Your mind has a bit more time to repeat, repeat, repeat the information as you are manually writing it down.

Say It Out Loud. Verbalizing the information that you are studying is another way to imbed it into your mind. Speaking the words aloud is like a double repetition, because you are simultaneously speaking them and hearing them. This involves your brain in yet another way, increasing the likelihood that you will remember the facts when you need them. As well, saying the words aloud actually teaches your mouth to recognize them. When you are trying to recall the information and can remember a phrase, whispering it tonics yourself can bring the entire piece of information right back into your mind.

Make Connections. Humor can be a useful tool to help you memorize a fact that just isn't sticking. Instead of looking at the information logically and intellectually, consider it in terms of associations or images. For example, let's say you are trying to learn the definition of 'scoliosis.' The word means curvature of the spine. You might notice that the letter's' occurs three times, and that this letter is a curvy one. It is also the first letter in the word 'spine.' When you see the word on a test, you will recognize the curving letters and remember the association with 'spine'!

When you create a strange association, your brain sees this as something out of the ordinary. The brain has a sense of humor, and enjoys making puns, putting together unusual images and otherwise having fun with language and ideas. It remembers things that are out of the ordinary more than it does the commonplace. So the more bizarre you make this combination, the better your chance of recalling the information.

Keep in mind that using only one of these suggestions in and of itself is not the ultimate key to memorization. If one of the techniques doesn't work for a particular bit of information, try another. You can even combine a couple of approaches. The more you use these strategies, the more likely your brain is to agree with you that the material you are studying is not only worth remembering, it is actually enjoyable.

Following are some additional strategies to help you memorize material. Try different ones and see what sticks the best for you.

Using Mnemonics

Mnemonics are tricks to help you remember information. Mnemonics come in several varieties, allowing you to choose what clicks for you. Some mnemonics enjoy widespread use because they are easy and effective, but you can always make up your own.

Visual Mnemonics– Visual mnemonics involve creating images that somehow suggest the information that is to be remembered. The image might be connected to the information in some logical way, or it can be completely unrelated. For example, if you are trying to remember that an event took place in Chillicothe, Ohio, you could visualize a cup of coffee sitting in a freezer (chilly coffee). Imaging a map of the state of Ohio on the coffee much will to help you in remembering that Chillicothe is in Ohio.

Visual mnemonics can be useful in learning another language as well. For example, rey is the Spanish word for king or monarch. Visualizing a crown with rays of light coming out from it reinforces the meaning with a mental image. The Spanish verb caminar means 'to walk,' so you could visualize an old El Camino model of car that is broken down, forcing you to walk.

Acronyms – Acronyms use the letters in a phrase or sentence to create an easy-to-remember word. A well-known example of this is ROY G. BIV. The letters stand for red, orange, yellow, green, blue, indigo and violet, which are the colors of the spectrum in order. This technique can be combined with a visual mnemonic to further lock it in. Imagining a cartoon character names Roy G. Biv, who wears a red hat, has orange hair, a yellow tie, a green shirt, a blue belt, indigo pants and a violet shirt makes the information you are trying to memorize impossible to forget!

A variation of the acronym mnemonic is to use the letters to create a simple sentence. In the case of the spectrum colors, 'Richard of York Gave Battle in Vain' can serve as a memory device. Creating a simple song to go along with a sentence mnemonic makes remembering the words a tad easier.

Here is an example for anyone who is studying biology and needs to know taxonomy classifications. By looking at the first letters of each word in the acronym 'Kids Prefer Cheese Over Fried Green Spinach,' it is easy to remember Kingdom, Phylum, Class, Order, Family, Genus, Species, and these are the taxonomy classifications in order.

Acronyms can be used for any subject, including math. For example, at first glance pi seems like a hopelessly long string of numbers that is nearly impossible to memorize. But the acronym 'How I wish I could calculate pi' is all you need to know. Here, the acronym isn't based upon the first letter of each word, but upon the number of letters in each word. The first word, 'how' has three letters. 'I' is a single letter, while 'wish' is a four-letter word. These are the first 3 numbers in pi—3.14. The number of letters in each word represents one digit of pi, giving you 3.141592. Memorizing a simple, fun phrase can save a lot of time and brain power.

Taking a Mnemonic Journey – Also known as the Method of Loci, journey mnemonics simply involve taking a mental journey with the information you are trying to integrate. As you study, imagine yourself walking through a familiar area. Picture words or images that represent the information superimposed on or featured in a particular location along the journey. For example, if you are studying art history, you might imagine yourself walking through your home, from the entrance to the bedroom. Throughout your walk, visualize famous paintings or sculptures along the walls, floor, or in the doorways. Take the mental walk a few times to really lock in the information. By mentally retracing those steps during the art history exam, the art work and artists will be easy to recall.

This method does not have to be used with paintings, sculptures or other obviously visual items. You can combine it with one or more other techniques and apply them to any subject.

Picturing something in a specific location that you know well will help reinforce the connection. For example, the crown with rays of light coming out of it may be hanging on your bedpost, while the El Camino is parked outside your window.

Word Play – Rhymes and catchy phrases are an excellent mnemonic approach for adults as well as for children. They do not have to be complicated and can be used for any subject. Some rhymes have been so ingrained in us that decades after learning them, they come back to help us remember how to spell a word or recall a fact. Remembering the spelling mnemonic, 'I before E, except after C, or when sounded like A, as in neighbor and weigh,' has helped many a child—and adult--manage difficult spelling challenges. Remembering the meanings of the homonyms 'there,' 'their,' and 'they're' is made easier by recalling the catchy phrase, " 'Here' is in 'there', 'heir' is in 'their', and they're just means they are.'" This one works because both 'here' and 'there' are locations, while 'their' refers to possession, and an 'heir' inherits possessions. You can create a little rhyme to explain all kinds of words you have trouble remembering how to spell. For example, 'There are three e's buried in the cemetery' helps unblock confusion about which vowel to use.

Associations – Another way to remember something is to associate the information with something easier to recall. While associations can be loosely grouped with other types of mnemonics, they are actually a little different. For example, many people have difficulty remembering the difference between stalactites and stalagmites. Stalactites grow down from the cave's ceiling, and there is a 'c' in the middle of the word. Stalagmites, however, contains a 'g', and since they grow up from the ground, that 'g' can stand for 'ground.' Confusing dessert and desert is a very common mistake, but it is easy to create an association to help you remember the difference. For example, the Sahara is a famous desert, and both words contain a single 's.' Another word for dessert is sweets, and both of those words contain two letters 's.'

Associations do not have to be based upon spelling. For a physical example on how associations can work, take a look at your hands. You are going to use the knuckles and the spaces between them as association points to the months in the year. Starting with your left pinky knuckle, name the months. The months that fall in the spaces between the knuckles have 30 days, except for February. Those that land on the knuckles are months can contain 31 days. For this trick to work, skip the valley between thumb and index fingers and jump to the right hand's index knuckle, since both July and August have 31 days. Another physical mnemonic useful for teaching youngsters how to remember which is their right hand and which the left involves forming an 'L' with the thumb and index finger of the left hand. The 'L' is going in the correct direction, so that is the left hand.

Memory tricks can make studying a much easier process, regardless of your age. They do not have to be logical, sensible or even related to your subject, and your favorites may not work for other people. The trick is to make sure the mnemonics you use are ones that work for you.

STUDENT TIP - MNEMONIC TECHNIQUES - MAKE UP THE MOST BIZARRE AND PERSONALIZED MNEMONIC DEVICES

Picture this, it's the night before a big test and you keep forgetting the same things. You are starting to panic now as you imagine staring at a failed test mark. So, you go to google and type the only logical thing you can think of, "best study hacks", and hit search. Of course, the first tip is to start a few weeks earlier and study a bit every day but that's not exactly helpful right now, especially because you have tried and still can't remember what year WWI ended or who invented the light bulb for the life of you. But don't worry because my favorite study tip is to make up the most bizarre and personalized mnemonic devices which will help you remember anything. I'm sure we have all heard of the basic ones such as BEDMAS to remember the order of operations in math, but those aren't always given to you, besides, acronyms are boring, so let me show you how I create the most outlandish mnemonic devices.

Let's start off with an example, in one of my junior science classes I had to remember who discovered the different parts of the atom. It was hard to remember the names and which parts of the atom they discovered and this is where my trick came into use. The scientist in question is J.J. Thomson. To me, that name sounds like a good name for a politician (my friends and family don't agree but that doesn't matter cause it is my tool!). People need to elect politicians which just so happens to sound like electrons. This helps me easily associate his name with the word electron and makes sense to me (which is the most important thing!)

STUDENT TIP - MNEMONICS TECHNIQUE EXAMPLE - HOW I DO IT

But how do you come up with these? Well, let's do one together and I will take you through my process. If you have taken grade 10 math you will know the terms, domain and range.

They describe the x and y values that are in a function/line.

But how am I supposed to remember which describes the x and which describes the y?

Assess the situation. Thankfully, this example is a binary so I only need a way of remembering one and can use the process of elimination to deduce the other.

Pick one. I am going to use range since I can think of more word associations for range than for domain.

State your objective. I have to remember that the range describes the y value.

List your associations, A.K.A. what comes to mind when you think of range. For me this is:

a. Distance

b. Free-range

c. Mountain range

Pick one of your associations and find other words to associate it with. Remember to keep in mind your end goal (which is y, in this case). If the first word you pick doesn't work, try the next.

a. Free-Range
b. Cattle/Cows
c. Cowboys
d. Chicken
e. Farms

Now try to make a connection between one of the words and y. The earlier you do this the easier it will be but some of the outlandish ones really stick in your brain!

a. Cowboys say yeehaw! What letter does that start with? Y!

Now string it all together. The range is like a cattle range, which has cowboys on it, who say yeehaw! This starts with the letter y and therefore the range determines the y values.

Mnemonic Technique 1 – Association

When I first heard of this, I thought of it as weird and odd but it eventually worked out in the end. Through the power of mental association, you have the ability to attach a word, person, or thing to foreign content as a means of helping you remember the information. As an example, in my chemistry class, the main way that I remembered that Krypton was one of the seven noble gases was by associating it with Superman's home planet which shares the same name.

Mnemonic Technique 2 – It Only has to Make Sense to You!

I use very silly word associations to remember everything from biological concepts to vocabulary words. For example, I recently had to memorize Spanish words, including the word "el reclamo," which means demand. I first noticed that it has the word "clam" in it, so I spent the entire time that I was studying saying to myself "the clam demands," and it worked. I also remembered the word "mermado" based on mermaids, and started associating the word "teachers" with "magic" to remember "elmagisterio."

I use this same strategy for more complex things like processes, which most people don't think works. For example, action potentials in neurons and the membranes of muscle cells are triggered by sodium, chemical symbol Na, entering the cell, and the process ends when potassium exits. I had trouble remembering which ion went in, and which went out. So, I wrote "Nain" and "Potout" in my notes. To me, that was a totally normal way to memorize that.

However, a friend of mine looked at my notes and asked if I'd had a stroke when writing it. Even after I explained what it meant, they still couldn't' believe that that gibberish meant anything to me, let alone helped me learn. I had never realized how differently my brain works, but since then, I've noticed it in a lot of things. For example, I do math much differently from other people.

For example, when adding in my head, I add however many it takes to get to the next multiple of 10, then subtract the number I just used.

Mnemonic Technique 3 – Study in Your own Way

Everyone studies in their own way and has their own strategies to excel, and now, I have one too. Rather than spend all day glued to my desk doing nothing, I study. I feel the need to clarify; no, I do not suddenly enjoy reading pages on pages about the Krebs cycle. However, I do make myself acronyms and mnemonics that make me laugh, and as a teeny tiny side effect, also remember what I need to about a certain topic.

For instance, let me explain to you how I memorize the Krebs cycle.

NaC, NaC, Ga, Fa, Na!

Try saying that out loud. Sounds like some sort of alien language, I know, but bear with me. A common question regarding the Krebs cycle, asks what the net energy production is, in a single cycle. Here is how I remember it. The 'Na' stands for NADH, the 'C' stands for CO_2, the 'Ga' stands for GTP, the 'Fa' stands for $FADH_2$. There are 3 'Na' in the mnemonic, telling me that 3 molecules of NADH are produced; the 2 'C' tells me that 2 molecules of 'CO_2' are produced; the single 'Ga' lets me know that 1 GTP molecule has been produced and the 'Fa' tells me that 1 molecule of $FADH_2$ has been produced.

NaC, NaC, Ga, Fa, Na!!

I do not feel the need to "study" all day for a test, because now when I do study, I also make myself laugh, which only further helps me understand and remember, and also keeps me engaged. Would you look at that; I have made the oh so boring Krebs cycle, significantly more bearable.

MEMORY PALACE TECHNIQUE WITH EXAMPLES

The Memory Palace Technique

The Memory Palace Technique creates stories with familiar places and objects which are associated with certain information. Let me explain the process, let's us an example to help simplify. We are going to memorize the number five hundred twenty two. To begin we pick a familiar location, for me I choose from my home, school, etc. Places you are familiar with and that you can "virtually walk through". We will choose my home for this example.

Choose A Start

Once the location is chosen you need to identify specific objects within that location. For example, we will choose the front door, and the piano. The first location, the front door will be associated with the first number (or desired information). The five will be associated with the door. Then we associate the five with something you understand (we will do the same with the 2's). Personally I associate 5 will my best friend and I giving each other a high 5. Allow me to take a step back and explain. As we begin to associate not only the number (5) with a person/action (my best friend and I high fiving) we are creating a story. Like I mentioned earlier the 5 is associated with the door. So in your mind you imagine standing at your front door giving a high 5 to your best friend. Now this piece of information is "backed up" by a place, person, and action. Choose actions/ people/ and places that you are familiar with. For me 5 and high fives associate, whenever I think of high fives I think of the number 5. For you it may be different. What matters is that without fail you'll remember!

Walk Around!

As we continue on we realize we still have the 22 of the 522 we need to memorize. Think back to where we identified the piano in the living. So in your mind we will "walk" from the front door where I'm giving my friend a high five to the piano. Now we need to associate 22 with a action. For me 22 is easily memorized by the song "22" by Taylor Swift. Accordingly, my mind story involves Taylor Swift singing 22 on my piano. So my mind story begins with me at my front door high fiving my friend. Then, walking to my piano where Taylor Swift sings 22. I then know I was memorizing 522, the 5 from the high five, and the 22 from the piano and Taylor Swift. Mind stories are limitless with how much information and "locations" you can add into a story.

Now this seems quite complicated and some may say that it's too much work to memorize. However, with practice comes perfection. It takes time to be able to associate certain information with these places, people, and actions. It takes effort to create mind stories.

Memorize The Steps Of Photosynthesis

For example, let's say that you wanted to remember the process of photosynthesis.

Use the Memory Palace Technique to memorize the steps of photosynthesis:

> **Step 1:** CO_2 and H_2O enter the leaf
>
> **Step 2:** Light hits the pigment in the membrane of a thylakoid, splitting the H_2O into O_2
>
> **Step 3:** The electrons move down to enzymes.
>
> **Step 4:** Sunlight hits the second pigment molecule allowing the enzymes to convert ADP to ATP and NADP+ gets converted to NADPH
>
> **Step 5:** The ATP and NADP is used by the Calvin cycle as a power source for converting carbon dioxide from the atmosphere into simple sugar glucose

Step 6: The Calvin cycle converts $3CO_2$ molecules from the atmosphere to glucose

Under normal circumstances, you may have just repeated the process in your head a hundred times. When the test day, comes and you are sitting in the classroom answering the question, you doubt yourself if the electrons moving down to enzymes was in step 3 or 5. You sweat and mentally cry about your studying method failing you.

However, if you were to use your memory palace, it would go something like this: (Bear with me, you do have to actively imagine what I say in your head for this to work)

First, imagine you are walking in a thick forest, and you come across this friendly cottage. Imagine that this house represents the "leaf". You are curious and want to enter the house, but it is locked. To "enter" the house, you carry two buckets filled with "CO_2" and "H_2O". The door opens, and you are in the living room. You set the two buckets onto the coffee table and noticed the intense afternoon "light" entering from the window and shining onto the two buckets. Out of surprise, you see the H_2O bucket slowly evaporating into "O_2". Before you can react, you are picked up by thousands of big-sized "electrons", and they carry you "down" to the hallway.

Memory Palace Technique For Anatomy & Physiology

Creating a memory palace is simply associating a name/fact or whatever you want to remember with a point in a room or building. If you have 25 things to remember you can come up with 25 points throughout your house and relate them together. Sometimes you create a story that flows from one to the other, sometimes they are isolated. I was studying college level Anatomy and Physiology at the time and decided to try it on the 12 pairs of cranial nerves. Since I was traveling, I decided to use my body as the "palace". Here is how it went.

I assigned 11 points on my body. Top of head, eyes, mouth,

ears, throat, shoulders, sternal notch (bottom of neck), chest, stomach, back pocket (ok, it was actually my butt), knees. I then assigned each cranial nerve, in order to these points in a way I could remember.

Olfactory nerve. I pictured an old factory sitting on top of my head, chugging away very black and toxic smoke. The Olfactory nerve transmits messages of smell to your brain.

Optic nerve. I pictured a pair of old fashioned glasses sitting part way down my nose. The Optic nerve innervates the eyes for sight.

Oculomotor nerve. Here I had an eyeball in between my lips. I would move my lips around (holding a "whistling" pose) to make the eyeball look around. The Oculomotor nerve relays motor nerve to eye for all but two eye muscles.

Trochlear nerve. Trochlear means "pulley". I had a pully attached to my shoulder, and pulling on the rope through the pulley moved my eyeball. Trochlear nerve feeds the superior oblique muscle of the eye.

Trigeminal nerve. I pictured three (tri) gem stones at the base of my neck, kind of in the shape of two eyes and round mouth. The Trigeminal nerve innervates parts of the face.

Abducens nerve. This was my shoulder. I pictured myself ramming my shoulder into someone's abdomen. Their eye popped out and was just hanging by one muscle. The lateral rectus muscle to be exact. Which is what this nerve innervates.

Facial nerve. I pictured a face shape pushing out of the skin of my chest. It was moving around making different facial expressions. The Facial nerve supplies sensory and motor nerves to muscles of facial expression, part of tongue, and some others.

Vestibulocochlear nerve. I envisioned myself dressed as a clown wearing a vest, balancing on a ball holding a can of coke. This nerve feeds the inner ear and is responsible for balance.

Glossopharyngeal nerve. This one involved a glossy potbelly with a big tongue hanging over it. It innervates parts of the tongue and back of the pharynx (throat).

Vagus nerve. This is a nerve I learned many years ago so I did not assign a position to it.

Accessory nerve. A bunch of accessory items hanging from my neck. I didn't want them swinging around so I stuck them into my back pocket. The Accessory nerve feeds the muscles in your neck.

Hypoglossal nerve. This was my knees. I am hyper and bouncing up and down on my knees on glossy fat tummy (to tie in with the 9th nerve). I also know that gloss is the root word for tongue. This nerve innervates parts of the tongue.

Using Flash Cards

If you remember going to school, then you remember flash cards. That much is certain, because almost every teacher for every student uses flash cards. And indeed, they have become such a staple in schools throughout the world that there is never a clear origin of their use. Wherever we find evidence of formal education, we find the use of flash cards.

There's a good reason. Flash cards work.

For the sake of definition, flashcards can be any cards, whether designed professionally or by a teacher. These cards contain information, such as math facts, words, historical facts, etc. Often they feature a question on one side with the answer on the other. Flashcards work by using repetition and association clues.

One of the most popular methods of flashcard use was developed in the 1970s by Sebastian Leitner, a German scientist. Under the Leitner system, the cards are arranged in groups according to how well the person knows each one in the learning box.

A short description of how it works: The student studies the material and then attempts to remember the solution, which is written on one of the card's sides. If the student recalls it correctly, the card is sent to the second group. If he does not remember it, the card goes back to the first group. Each next group of cards has a longer duration of time before the student is required to revisit those cards.

The Leitner System works effectively because of the principle of spaced repetition, which it utilizes. Other names for The Leitner System are The Leitner Method, The Leitner Principle, The Leitner Card box System, or the Leitner Card file System.

The concept is that, if a student finds it easy to remember the material on a card, then his learning time should not be focused as much on that card, and so in the future the study of that card is repeated less often. The reverse is also true. If the student finds it difficult to remember material on a card, then it must studied more often. Each card's study time is spaced or scheduled in a way so that he or she spends most study time with the more challenging material. The material that was learned well is still revisited from time to time, but only briefly, and only to make sure the student has not forgotten it.

Let's look at how these principles are actually executed on a practical level. First, set up a card-box or card file to hold the cards. This container has several compartments inside of it (sometimes called "decks").

Each card starts in compartment or deck 1. After you recall the material on the flashcard correctly, move the card to the next deck, or deck 2. In future sessions, if cards in deck 2 seem not to be remembered well, move them back to deck 1. There can also be a deck 3, deck 4, and so on, with you determining how well you need to know the card to advance to the next deck or compartment. Even if a card has made it all the way to a third or fourth compartment, if in the future it appears not to be recalled well, move it all the way back to the first deck and start the process again.

You can determine how long you can wait to review the cards in each deck. For instance, since deck 1 contains the material that has not been learned well, there is no day that can be skipped before a review; those cards are studied every day. The cards in deck 2 have been learned well enough that you are allowed to skip 1 day. Those in deck 3, you can skip studying for 3 days; those in deck 4, you can skip for 7 days; and those in deck 5, you may skip for a month before reviewing.

The Leitner system, in short, takes the best aspects of the flashcard method of learning and hones it to both a science and an art.

MORE TIPS FOR FLASH CARDS

There is no need to buy flash cards because they are easy to make. Making your own also ensures that your flash cards include the information that you need to know. Flash cards can be made out of index cards, sheets from note pads, or pieces of paper cut into squares. It is not necessary that they are all the same size and shape, but it helps when storing, sorting and organizing.

• Choose the most important facts from lectures, notes or your text to write on your flash cards. Unless you are required to learn a specific definition, put the information in your own words.

• Label your flash cards with the subject and date. This helps you categorize them for different quizzes and tests.

There are several ways of organizing information on the flash cards, depending on what type of information you are studying:

• Terms: Put the word on one side of the card and the definition on the other. Include examples that help clarify the definition.

• Mathematics: Put problems on one side and answers on the other. Include the steps for solving the problem and any illustrations that help make the answer clear.

• You can also draw pictures on one side, with an arrow pointing to what you need to know, with the answer on the other side. This method is helpful when studying maps, places and anatomy.

You can study with flash cards in several ways:

• Look at the problem side of the card and answer it. You can check your answer by looking at the other side.

• For terms, you can alter your study method by looking at the answer and trying to name the term that goes with it. This method will also work with image flash cards.

• Make studying with flash cards a game. As you answer for each card, place it into either the "I knew it" pile or the "I didn't know it" pile. When you get to the end, pick up the "I didn't know it" pile, shuffle them and start over. It will not take long for the "I didn't know it" pile to get smaller. After a few days, that pile will be non-existent.

• Use the flash cards every day for 5 to 10 minutes. They are small and portable, so you can pull out the flash cards for a quick cram session anywhere.

• When you have cards that you know every time and that require no hesitation, take them out of the deck. Replace them with new cards that have more difficult information. The replaced cards can be used for a quick review session the night before an exam.

Flash cards are small and portable, making them a study aid that you can use any time in any place. They may remind of you of learning mathematics in grade school, but there was a reason teachers always insisted on using them. They are an easy, effective and inexpensive way to learn any subject in a few minutes per day.

MINDFULNESS - A TOP STUDY METHOD

Doing well on exams may not be enough anymore. You need to graduate with marks that wow, dazzle and sparkle. Standardized testing is currently how comparisons are made among schools and between students. As a student you are in control of yourself and how well you can do on an exam.

Mindfulness is having your mind "full" of the present moment. In other words being present in the moment and fully attending to what you are doing by using your senses. Here is a list of mindfulness studying techniques to assist you in feeling confident and prepared for your examinations.

Step 1. Mindfulness/Meditation

Mindfulness/Meditation- Improves focus by causing an increase in cortical thickness in regions of the brain responsible for attention. Increases dopamine and serotonin levels which are associated with happiness and positivity. Decreases stress and anxiety by creating a state of relaxation causing breathing, pulse, and blood pressure to decrease.

Incorporate into your studies:

1) Scan and observe your body. What do you need right now? Are you hungry, thirsty, or is t-shirt tag scratching the back of you neck?

2) Use any breathing technique for one minute. Ex. 4 square breathing. Slow your thoughts. Think about being attentive, non-judgmental and curious about your studies. Notice your thoughts and how they impact your studies. Accept the positive thoughts and let the negative worries float away.

Step 2. Set A Timer And Focus

Set a timer for 30 minutes and focus solely on your studies. While you study sit at a desk. Use the pen or pencil you will use during the test. You could even wear the same outfit every time you study, as you will wear during the test. Train your brain. When I wear this or use this I am thinking about my exam.

Step 3. Visual Perception

Visual Perception is how the brain processes impulses- recognizing, differentiating and interpreting visual stimuli through comparison with experiences made earlier in life.

Incorporate into your studies:

1) READ!

2) Create mind maps. It is a great way to break down information into a simple diagram that can be learned and remembered easily.

3) Write down questions and answer them later.

Step 4 - Sound

Hearing is how the brain perceives sounds.

Incorporate into your studies:

1) Listen to an audio recording on the topic. While listening write down key notes on what is being said to help you better understand the subject.

2) Read out loud to yourself.

3) Teach the topic to someone else. Be mindful and aware of what you are saying.

Step 5. Vestibular

Vestibular is the perception of our body in relation to gravity, movement and balance.

Incorporate into your studies:

> 1) Use alternative seating. It is an effective strategy to facilitate the nervous system in regulating arousal and staying focused. Ex. Seat cushions, standing, wiggle chairs.

Step 6. Take Breaks

When your timer goes off TAKE A BREAK. Have an incentive. Go for a walk and get fresh air. Rest your eyes and hand.

> "Studying doesn't suck nearly as much as failing or re-doing." Unknown

CLUSTERING

The Science-Backed Method of Information
Simplification

Here it is: Information clustering. To get a good grade, you could memorize everything and then use as much or as little as you need for each question... but we all know that isn't very practical. A better approach is to cluster or clump small bits of information together so you can easily remember which ideas go with which (for example, categorizing fruits vs vegetables – don't forget, tomatoes are fruits!). Simplifying the information makes it a lot easier to remember later and with a lot less frustration, tears, and 'I can't do it's. But don't leave out all the details! This is the study method that helped propel my grades from 60s and 70s to high 80s and 90s:

Simple → Complex → Simple

Start With Easy

First, begin with simple, easy-to-understand information.

Then, build to complex, detailed information.

Finally, re-simplify the information so you can remember the general ideas no problem, and cue your own memory for the difficult stuff.

On test day, instead of racking your brain for information that may or may not be there – or even worse, feeling like you just can't grasp what you're looking for, even though you know it is there – you can calmly organize your thoughts and let the answers flow. It's like filling in a crossword puzzle: As more words are entered, it gets easier and easier to recognize what is missing.

For this approach, there are five easy-peasy, quick-and-simple (yet effective!) steps:

Simple → Complex → Simple

Consult the syllabus – yes, they really can be useful!

Trust me, that course outline might seem like a waste of paper, but it will really help you get an idea of the extent of the course's material. Plus, how much simpler can it get?? Sometimes just reading the order that the chapters are covered in can give you a broader sense of how the material will progress. No more questions like, 'When will I ever use this again??' (the answer might be: Next week!). In most of my university courses, later chapters required a concrete understanding of the earlier ones. Stay on top of things from the beginning and it will be a much smoother ride.

Get The Textbook

Refer to the textbook – please don't read the whole thing!

Now that you have flawless notes, use them as a guide for your studying. If there is something you don't quite understand or that isn't easy to remember, the textbook can be a saving grace. Imagine it like a story book: Each chapter is filled with storylines surrounding each of the main topics of the course. The textbook can give you context surrounding the ideas in your notes, which can be a lot easier to remember than just lists or bullet points of information. If you feel you already have a good grasp on an idea, skip that section! In general, I find it's more beneficial to understand a wide range of simple concepts than only a few very detailed areas of a test. (Partial points, my friend! It all adds up!)

Simple → Complex → Simple

Summarize the ideas – keep it short and sweet!

Now that you have a broader understanding of the information, it's time to break it back down. I don't know about you, but being overwhelmed with details going into a test usually ends up in me drawing a complete blank. Don't waste all that hard work! This is the part where highlighters, colour-coding, and sketching usually come into play. Whatever works for you, simplify the details into basic concepts. Quick outlines of important diagrams or charts can help with remembering the more complex versions. Bullet points can really help shorten long paragraphs into manageable pieces. Remember, keep it short and sweet!

Cluster!

Cluster the information – easy-peasy!

Now here's the game changer: Instead of stopping at the summary, really break those ideas down into bite-sized pieces. And I mean super simple – try to put each idea or piece of information into one word. Then, cluster those words into categories (concepts) so you can easily remember which ideas belong together. Clustering is a science-based way to easily remember complex information (thank-you psychology!). Typically, I find 4-6 words per cluster works best, with lots of symbols and shorthand.

Here are three examples of clusters from my dreaded Neurobiology course (which I got an A+ in, thanks to this method!):

Graded potentials

Dendrites

EPSP ↑ AP

IPSP ↓ AP

Action potential

Axons

Resting potential (↓)

Depolarization (↑)

Potential spike (↑↑)

Hyperpolarization (↓↓)

Conduction properties

Myelination

Insulation

Saltatory conduction

Nodes of Ranvier

And that's all there is to it! Yes, there is a bit of work in-volved... but that's a bit of a given, and it will all pay off in the end. The biggest benefit of this method for me has been the amount of information I still remember even after the test is over. This has been especially helpful for getting into a research position and feeling confident during final exams. Breaking things down and taking the time to understand the course material properly the first time saves a lot of time and energy that might otherwise go into re-learning it or cram-ming the night before! And hey, it's backed by science... so what's not to love?

Tips from Students

1. Learn 80%
This may be a controversial tactic, but it was key to my test preparation. My goal was to only learn 80% of the material I needed. I didn't actually measure out exactly 80%, but if I didn't understand something after struggling with it for a while, I simply wouldn't learn it. This made my test prepara-tion more efficient and took a lot of pressure off my shoul-ders. No one can learn 100% of everything!

2. Get creative to prevent boredom
I'm a busy body, and I find sitting for eight hours exhaust-ing. So my study method and schedule included a lot of non-sitting studying. For instance, I would watch MCAT content videos on my iPad while on the elliptical and listen to relevant podcasts while walking my dog. This allowed me to prevent boredom and continue learning.

3. Practice the test in a simulated environment

I can't overstate how important it was for me to practice the whole test beforehand. The MCAT was a marathon, so practice helped to train my brain's endurance, my familiarity with what to expect, and to move onto the next question without looking back.

4. Use verbal questions and answers for your self-tests

Purpose: This way you are conscious of the specific information. The mind associates well with goals, and a question forms a goal, which can help stimulate the mind.

When not to use words: If the material is visually related, your answers should be visual, represented in drawings. If you are doing a self-test on a skill, formulate a problem and use acquired skills to solve.

Question the material by asking yourself "why or how does this make any sense?" then find answers to the questions to improve memory.

You may have used these form of questioning during your first reading when you tried to understand the material. Using it now is to help you form more strong associations to build your memory. The question is not a form of self-test. A self-test question should be more specific and answers should provide more information than answering why something sounds reasonable to you.

Rearrange two more related bits or chinks of information, study them and form self-test questions

Arrange chunks of information as you expect they would appear in a real test, or applicable real-life situations.

Purpose: Your memory of target information is quite sensitive to the learning sequence. For example, if you studied Point 1 and used Point 1 to trigger Point 2, but face a test question that request you recall Point 1, your memory which is based on your learning sequence will not begin by considering Point 2 as a trigger for Point 1.

Good Study Habits and Useful Tips

There are several ways to improve your studying that don't fit neatly into a category. Take a look at these and see what you can use.

Books on Tape

Listening to a tape in which someone reads a book is a great way to take in the information from a book when you're short on time. You can find books on tape at the library as well as some bookstores and record stores. The advantage of listening to these books is that they are typically a high quality sound with a professional actor reading the script. And you can listen to the content of an assigned reading while you eat lunch, clean your room or even while you're driving.

Spend your time wisely

It's important to get a feel for your teacher and figure out her style and her priorities. This can give you an indication as to what will be on the test, so that you don't waste time on material that's irrelevant.

Should I do extra credit assignments?

You should always take advantage of extra credit assignments. Don't turn your back on a chance to boost your term mark by ignoring this great opportunity. Taking the time to do extra credit assignments shows your teacher that you are committed to your school work and can affect your final grade when the teacher is deciding on a mark. If she sees you've put in extra effort she may choose to bump up a lower mark.

And those extra few points you earned from an extra credit assignment could be the difference between you the other students in the class when it comes to determining the top student in the class.

Why shortcuts are a waste of time

You may think you are saving time with shortcuts, but in the long run, they are almost always not worth those extra few minutes. Doing shortcuts when it comes to assignments often leaves you unprepared for an upcoming test. You just can't take in all the required material if you don't complete the whole assignment. A shortcut could mean the difference between an A or a B on a test or even the term mark.

Be on time

Make sure you always hand your homework assignments in by the due date. You'll not only ensure you won't lose points on the assignment, you'll also make sure you don't fall behind as the class goes on to the next thing.

Have a positive frame of mind

A positive self-image is important in academic success. In fact how you perceive yourself will affect how you manage your time. See yourself as a success and you are more likely to achieve that success. Expect to make A's and you have a better chance at getting that mark. But if you are sure you'll fail the course you will have a harder time motivating yourself to study. You can set yourself up for failure if you have the wrong frame of mind.

So use your imagination and picture yourself doing well, and really getting a lot out of study time. Create a clear vision in your head of you studying productively. The next step is to follow through with that vision.

See yourself succeeding

You can create an effective study plan by first picturing the work that you are required to do and making a conscious plan to complete it. Organize all of your assignments in front of you. Make a list of them. Then assign each assignment a specific time within your week. Then picture yourself actually completing these assignments at that assigned time, whether that is a picture of you going to the library or working in your room. The important thing is to make a plan, and then visualize yourself successfully completing that plan.

This plan of action is most effective if you create vivid details in the mental pictures you create. So visualize doing specific assignment tasks at particular times in a definite place.

How to Prepare for a Test

MOST STUDENTS HIDE THEIR HEADS AND PROCRASTINATE WHEN FACED WITH PREPARING FOR AN EXAM, HOPING THAT SOMEHOW THEY WILL BE SPARED THE AGONY, ESPECIALLY IF IT IS A BIG ONE THAT THEIR FUTURES RELY ON. Avoiding a test is what many students do best and unfortunately, they suffer the consequences because of their lack of preparation.

Test preparation requires strategy and dedication. It is the perfect training ground for a professional life. Besides having several reliable strategies, successful students also has a clear goal and know how to accomplish it. These tried and true concepts have worked well and will make your test preparation easier.

Test Prep and Study Skills Video Tutorials

https://www.test-preparation.ca/video-series-on-test-preparation-multiple-choice-strategies-and-how-to-study/

Take responsibility for your own test preparation.

It is a common - but big - mistake to link your studying to someone else's. Study partners are great, but only if they are reliable. It is your job to be prepared for the test, even if a study partner fails you. Do not allow others to distract you from your goals.

Prioritize the time available to study

When do you learn best, early in the day or at night? Does

your mind absorb and retain information most efficiently in small blocks of time, or do you require long stretches to get the most done? It is important to figure out the best blocks of time available to you when you can be the most productive. Try to consolidate activities to allow for longer periods of study time.

Find a quiet place where you will not be disturbed

Do not try to squeeze in quality study time in any old location. Find a quiet place with a minimum of distractions, such as the library, a park or even the laundry room. Good lighting is essential and you need to have comfortable seating and a desk surface large enough to hold your materials. It is probably not a great idea to study in your bedroom. You might be distracted by clothes on the floor, a book you have been planning to read, the telephone or something else. Besides, in the middle of studying, that bed will start to look very comfortable. Whatever you do, avoid using the bed as a place to study since you might fall asleep to avoiding studying!

The exception is flashcards. By far the most productive study time is sitting down and studying and studying only. However, with flashcards you can carry them with you and make use of odd moments, like standing in line or waiting for the bus. This isn't as productive, but it really helps and is definitely worth doing.

Determine what you need to study

Gather together your books, your notes, your laptop and any other materials needed to focus on your study for this exam. Ensure you have everything you need so you don't waste time. Remember paper, pencils and erasers, sticky notes, bottled water and a snack. Keep your phone with you if you need it to find essential information, but keep it turned off so others can't distract you.

Have a positive attitude

It is essential that you approach your studies for the test with an attitude that says you will pass it. And pass it with flying colors! This is one of the most important keys to successful studying. Believing that you are capable helps you to become capable.

THE STRATEGY OF STUDYING

Review class notes

Stay on top of class notes and assignments by reviewing them frequently and regularly and regularly. Re-writing notes can be a terrific study trick, as it helps lock in information. Pay special attention to any comments that have been made by the teacher. If a study guide has been made available as part of the class materials, use it! It will be a valuable tool to use for studying.

Estimate how much time you will need

If you are concerned about how much time you have available it is a good idea to set up a schedule so that you do not get bogged down on one section and end without enough time left to study other things. Remember to schedule breaks, and use that time for a little exercise or other stress reducing techniques.

Test yourself to determine your weaknesses

Look online for additional assessment and evaluation tools available like practice questions for a particular subject. Visit our website https://www.test-preparation.ca

What Students Say!

Visit our Online Library of student tips and strategies https://www.test-preparation.ca/test-prep-and-studying-what-students-say/
for test tips and more practice questions. Once you have de-

termined your weaknesses, you can focus on these, and just brush up on the other areas of the exam.

MENTAL PREP – HOW TO PSYCH YOURSELF UP FOR A TEST

Since tests are often a big factor in your final grade or acceptance into a program, it is understandable taking tests is stressful for many students. Even students who know they have learned the required material find their minds going blank as they stare at the test booklet. You can avoid test anxiety by preparing yourself mentally. One easy way to overcome that anxiety is to prepare mentally for the test with a few simple techniques.

Do not procrastinate

Study the material for the test when it becomes available, and continue to review the material until the test day. By waiting until the last minute and trying to cram for the test the night before, you actually increase anxiety. This leads to negative self-talk, which becomes self-fulfilling. Telling yourself "I can't learn this. I am going to fail" is a pretty sure indication that you are right.

Positive self-talk.

Positive self-talk drowns out negative self-talk and to increases your confidence level. Whenever you begin feeling overwhelmed or anxious about the test, remind yourself that you have studied enough, you know the material and that you will pass the test. Both negative and positive self-talk are really just your fantasy, so why not choose to be a winner?

Do not compare yourself to others.

Do not compare yourself to other students. Instead, focus on your strengths and weaknesses and prepare accordingly. Regardless of how others perform, your performance is the only one that effects your grade. Comparing yourself to others increases your anxiety and negative self-talk before the test.

Visualize.

Make a mental image of yourself taking the test. You know the answers and feel relaxed. Visualize doing well on the test and having no problems with the material. Visualizations can increase your confidence and decrease the anxiety you might otherwise feel before the test. Instead of thinking of this as a test, see it as an opportunity to demonstrate what you have learned!

Avoid negativity.

Worry is contagious and viral - once it gets started it builds on itself. Cut it off before it gets to be a problem. Even if you are relaxed and confident, being around anxious, worried classmates might cause you to start feeling anxious. Before the test, tune out the fears of classmates. Feeling anxious and worried before an exam is normal, and every student experiences those feelings at some point. But you cannot allow these feelings to interfere with your performance. Practicing mental preparation techniques and remembering that the test is not the only measure of your academic performance will ease your anxiety and ensure that you perform at your best.

WHAT YOUR PROFESSOR WANTS TO SEE ON YOUR EXAM

It sounds like such an easy question: "What does your instructor or teacher want to see from you on your test paper?" And the easy answer: "He wants to see the right answers."

TIPS

1. Get to know your instructors. Introduce yourself so that they know you and are aware that the course is vital to you. Make yourself visible – sit near the front of the class and attend regularly.

2. Give feedback. Everyone needs feedback on how they are doing! This helps instructors know what you like and want you want featured more during classes. Some instructors provide forums for periodic evaluations of their performance in the classroom. Make sure your fill them and let your instructors know what they can do to improve classroom performance.

3. Compliment instructors. When your lecturer or instructor gives a good demonstration or lecture, be sure to compliment them and let them know that you liked it and found it effective. Don't overdue it though and don't ingratiate yourself – be honest and authentic.

4. Keep the channels of communication open. Feel free to ask questions so that you are sure that you understand what the instructor requires. Participate in class discussions.

5. Ask for help when you need it. Don't be shy requesting help or clarification when you need it. The instructor would be happy to clarify or explain what you do not understand or find clear. Just be sure to ask pleasantly and respectfully that the instructor explains or restate an unclear point. Especially during classes, if you don't understand something, then chances are that others don't either. Most professors are very much aware of this.

6. Answer questions posed by your instructors. This encourages your instructor, shows your intelligence and stimulates your thinking. Lectures are prepared to stimulate students thinking. Refusing or ignoring to answer the questions won't help you or the instructor.

7. Take responsibility of your education. Don't be quick to request for extra considerations or favors from your instructors. Stop making excuses and take ownership of your learning by doing what has to be done when they have to be done. Instructors are not special humans and so have their off days and their own share of mistakes. Their job is not to entertain students and you cannot expect them to always be available to be your private instructors.

8. Show your instructor that you recognize and comprehend key concepts from the course. Sure, you can get that "A" by just answering the right questions. But showing your teacher that you understand what he has been teaching will make him more likely to help you in the future, and to give you the benefit of a doubt when a grade is in question. So especially on essay portions, do your best to explains in such a way that demonstrate that you have a true understanding of the course, and that you're not just regurgitating word-for-word what the book said.

9. Show him that you have neat handwriting and an organized presentation. No, it's not essential that your paper look good when you turn in your test. However, it does make a good impression. Perhaps more importantly, when the paper is neat, it's easier for the instructor to grade it. And when the paper is neat and easy to read, there's less chance of the instructor marking something wrong that should be marked right.

10. Show all work. This is especially true when it's a math exam. Even if you can figure out the answer in your head, unless it's a timed exam, you should show your work. There are two good reasons for this. First, as we've already mentioned, it's smart to make a good impression on the teacher, and to show that you truly grasp the material. On a more practical level, though, it also proves conclusively that you're not cheating on the test–that the test you're turning in is really your own.

11. Show him a paper that is free of personal bias and that sticks to fact. This is, of course, unless the question specifically asks for your opinion. Too many people, on a test that should be all fact, insert lots of opinion, especially into essay portions. They do this, often, to try to take the instructors' focus off the fact that the student doesn't know the facts of the course. This strategy almost never works.

12. Show good vocabulary. Most teachers are suckers for a student who uses an uncommon word in the correct way, when it's exactly the right word for the circumstance. It shows intelligence and that you're somebody who is genuinely learning.

13. Avoid flowery language. Using good vocabulary is one thing. Throwing in one difficult word after another, though, in order to sound more intelligent than you are comes across as fake. And it does not make a good impression. Remember: When it comes to using uncommon vocabulary words on an exam, moderation is the key. Use a few good words, but otherwise, use words that you would use in your everyday speech.

14. Similarly, use statistics when appropriate. Memorize some appropriate stats that pertain to the chapter that you're testing on, and when you find the right opportunity, cite those stats, to really show the instructor that you know the material.

15. Proofread your work before you turn in your paper. While most of our suggestions here have pertained to making a good impression in the instructor, it's also important that you not make a bad impression. For instance, papers that are filled with spelling or grammatical errors will not look good with most teachers. So make sure you re-read your paper before you turn it in, and correct any blatant errors in spelling or grammar that you see.

16. Follow the direction. It's amazing how many students know the material that's on the test, but they irritate the instructor by not following the directions given on the test paper. For instance, maybe the directions say to circle the correct answer, and the careless student underlines it. Or the directions state that it's a "True or False" section and the student answers "Yes or No." Not good–and not something that will have your instructor feeling good about you as a careful student.

17. **Finally, remember when you take a test that timing is important.** Some students rush through the exam, because they have to be the first person to finish. They think that it's a competition, and that the first person who finishes wins. However, this often communicates to the instructor that you were in a hurry and that you were likely careless in taking the test. On the other hand, waiting until you're the very last person to finish the test sends a subtle message that you were unsure of yourself. Try to be somewhere in the middle when you hand in your completed exam. If you get done too much

before everyone else, use that extra time to thoroughly proofread the test and check your answers.

These suggestions will set you apart above others in your class. They will turn your test into a tool that links you with your instructor, and puts him in your corner.

How to Take a Test

EVERYONE KNOWS THAT TAKING AN EXAM IS STRESSFUL, BUT IT DOES NOT HAVE TO BE THAT BAD! There are a few simple things that you can do to increase your score on any type of test. Take a look at these tips and consider how you can incorporate them into your study time.

OK - so you are in the test room - Here is what to do!

Student Tip

Chill, Check, Countdown

The intention of the 'day-of' should be to keep it chill, now stress will only hinder you. Check you've got all your supplies and then grab a coffee on your walk to the test in your favorite confidence boosting outfit. Showing up early is important, but sometimes it can get a little crazy with other students stressing and clarifying things with you that you didn't even know you had to study – and often aren't on the test anyway. In the countdown, depending on your preference, you could chill outside on a chair until it's time, or you just could walk in. Now is your time to shine!

Reading the Instructions

This is the most basic point, but one that, surprisingly, many students ignore and it costs big time! Since reading the instructions is one of the most common, and 100% preventable mistakes, we have a whole section just on reading instructions.

Pay close attention to the sample questions. Almost all standardized tests offer sample questions, paired with their correct solutions. Go through these to make sure that you understand what they mean and how they arrived at the correct answer. Do not be afraid to ask the test supervisor for help with a sample that confuses you, or instructions that you are unsure of.

Tips for Reading the Question

We could write pages and pages of tips just on reading the test questions. Here are a few that will help you the most.

- **Think first.** Before you look at the answer, read and think about the question. It is best to try to come up with the correct answer before you look at the options. This way, when the test-writer tries to trick you with a close answer, you will not fall for it.

- **Make it true or false.** If a question confuses you, then look at each answer option and think of it as a "true" "false" question. Select the one that seems most likely to be "true."

- **Mark the Question.** Don't be afraid to mark up the test booklet. Unless you are specifically told not to mark in the booklet, use it to your advantage.

- **Circle Key Words.** As you are reading the question, underline or circle key words. This helps you to focus on the most critical information needed to solve the problem. For example, if the question said, "Which of these is not a synonym for huge?" You might circle "not," "synonym" and "huge." That clears away the clutter and lets you focus on what is important.

- **Always underline these words:** all, none, always, never, most, best, true, false and except.

- **Eliminate.** Elimination is the best strategy for multiple choice answers *and* questions. If you are confused by lengthy questions, cross out anything that you think is irrelevant, obviously wrong, or information that you think is offered to distract you. Elimination is the most valuable strategy!

- **Do not try to read between the lines.** Usually, questions are written to be straightforward, with no deep, underlying meaning. Generally, the simple answer really is the correct answer. Do not over-analyze!

How to Take a Test - The Basics

Some sections of the test are designed to assess your ability to quickly grab the necessary information; this type of exam makes speed a priority. Others are more concerned with your depth of knowledge, and how accurate it is. When you start a new section of the test, look it over to determine whether the test is for speed or accuracy. If the test is for speed (a lot of questions and a short time), your strategy is clear; answer as many questions as quickly as possible.

Make time your friend

Budget your time from the beginning until you are finished, and stick to it! The time for each section will be included in the instructions.

Easy does it

One smart way to tackle a test is to locate the easy questions and answer those first. This is a time-tested strategy that never fails, because it saves you a lot of unnecessary anxiety. First, read the question and decide if you can answer it in less than a minute. If so, complete the question and go to the next one. If not, skip it for now and continue to the next question. By the time you have completed the first pass through this section of the exam, you will have answered a good number of questions. Not only does it boost your confidence, relieve anxiety and kick your memory up a notch, you will know exactly how many questions remain and can allot the rest of your time accordingly. Think of doing the easy questions first as a warm-up!

Do not watch your watch

At best, taking an important exam is an uncomfortable situation. If you are like most people, you might be tempted to subconsciously distract yourself from the task at hand. One of the most common ways is by becoming obsessed with your watch or the wall clock. Do not watch your watch! Take it off and place it on the top corner of your desk, far enough away that you will not be tempted to look at it every two minutes. Better still, turn the watch face away from you. That way, every time you try to sneak a peek, you will be reminded to refocus your attention to the task at hand. Give yourself permission to check your watch or the wall clock after you complete each section. Focus on answering the questions, not on how many minutes have elapsed since you last looked at it.

Divide and conquer

What should you do when you come across a question that is so complicated you may not even be certain what is being asked? As we have suggested, the first time through, skip the question. At some point, you will need to return to it and get it under control. The best way to handle questions that leave you feeling so anxious you can hardly think is by breaking them into manageable pieces. Solving smaller bits is always easier. For complicated questions, divide them into bite-sized pieces and solve these smaller sets separately. Once you understand what the reduced sections are really saying, it will be much easier to put them together and get a handle on the bigger question. This may not work with every question - see below for how to deal with questions you cannot break down.

Reason your way through the toughest questions

If you find that a question is so dense you can't figure out how to break it into smaller pieces, there are a few strategies that might help. First, read the question again and look for hints. Can you re-word the question in one or more different ways? This may give you clues. Look for words that can function as either verbs or nouns, and try to figure out what the questions is asking from the sentence structure. Remember that many nouns in English have several different meanings. While some of those meanings might be related, sometimes they are completely distinct. If reading the sentence one way does not make sense, consider a different definition or meaning for a key word.

The truth is, it is not always necessary to understand a question to arrive at a correct answer! The most successful strategy for multiple choice is Elimination. Frequently, at least one answer is clearly wrong and can be crossed off the list of possible correct answers. Next, look at the remaining answers and eliminate any that are only partially true. You may still have to flat-out guess from time to time, but using the process of elimination will help you make your way to the correct answer more often than not - even when you don't know what the question means!

Do not leave early

Use all the time allotted to you, even if you can't wait to get out of the testing room. Instead, once you have finished, spend the remaining time reviewing your answers. Go back to those questions that were most difficult for you and review your response. Another good way to use this time is to return to multiple-choice questions in which you filled in a bubble. Do a spot check, reviewing every fifth or sixth question to make sure your answer coincides with the bubble you filled in. This is a great way to catch yourself if you made a mistake, skipped a bubble and therefore put all your answers in the wrong bubbles!

Become a super sleuth and look for careless errors. Look for questions that have double negatives or other odd phrasing;

they might be an attempt to throw you off. Careless errors on your part might be the result of skimming a question and missing a key word. Words such as "always," "never," "sometimes," "rarely" and the like can give a strong indication of the answer the question is really seeking. Don't throw away points by being careless!

Just as you budgeted time at the beginning of the test to allow for easy and more difficult questions, be sure to budget sufficient time to review your answers. On essay questions and math questions where you are required to show your work, check your writing to make sure it is legible.

Math questions can be especially tricky. The best way to double check math questions is by figuring the answer using a different method, if possible.
Here is another terrific tip. It is likely that no matter how hard you try, you will have a handful of questions you just are not sure of. Keep them in mind as you read through the rest of the test. If you can't answer a question, looking back over the test to find a different question that addresses the same topic might give you clues.

We know that taking the test has been stressful and you can hardly wait to escape. Just Leaving before you double-check as much as possible can be a quick trip to disaster. Taking a few extra minutes can make the difference between getting a bad grade and a great one. Besides, there will be lots of time to relax and celebrate after the test is turned in.

In the Test Room – What you MUST do!

If you are like the rest of the world, there is almost nothing you would rather avoid than taking a test. Unfortunately, that is not an option if you want to pass. Rather than suffer, consider a few attitude adjustments that might turn the experience from a horrible one to...well, an interesting one! Take a look at these tips. Simply changing how you perceive the experience can change the experience itself.

You have to take the test - you can't change that. What you can change, and the only thing that you can change, is your attitude -so get a grip - you can do it!

Get in the mood

After weeks of studying, the big day has finally arrived. The worst thing you can do is arrive at the test site feeling frustrated, worried, and anxious. Keep a check on your emotional state. If your emotions are shaky before a test it can determine how well you do on the test. It is extremely important that you pump yourself up, believe in yourself, and use that confidence to get in the mood!

Don't fight reality

Students often resent tests, and with good reason. After all, many people do not test well, and they know the grade they end with does not accurately reflect their true knowledge. It is easy to feel resentful because tests classify students and create categories that just don't seem fair. Face it: Students who are great at rote memorization and not that good at actually analyzing material often score higher than those who might be more creative thinkers and balk at simply memorizing cold, hard facts. It may not be fair, but there it is anyway. Conformity is an asset on tests, and creativity is often a liability. There is no point in wasting time or energy being upset about this reality. The first step is to accept the reality and get used to it. You will get higher marks when you realize tests do count and that you must give them your best effort. Think about your future and the career that is easier to achieve if you have consistently earned high grades. Avoid negative energy and focus on anything that lifts your enthusiasm and increases your motivation.

Get there early enough to relax

If you are tense, scared, anxious, or feeling rushed, it will cost you. Get to the exam room early and relax before you go in. This way, when the exam starts, you are comfortable and ready to apply yourself. Of course, you do not want to arrive so early that you are the only one there. That will not help you relax; it will only give you too much time to sit there, worry and get wound up all over again.

If you can, visit the room where you will be taking your exam a few days ahead of time. Having a visual image of the room can be surprisingly calming, because it takes away one of the big 'unknowns'. Not only that, but once you have visited, you know how to get there and will not be worried about getting lost. Furthermore, driving to the test site once lets you know how much time you need to allow for the trip. That means three potential stressors have been eliminated all at once.

Get it down on paper

One advantage of arriving early is that it allows you time to recreate notes. If you spend a lot of time worrying about whether you will be able to remember information like names, dates, places, and mathematical formulas, there is a solution for that. Unless the exam you are taking allows you to use your books and notes, (and very few do) you will have to rely on memory. Arriving early gives to time to tap into your memory and jot down key pieces of information you know that will be asked. Just make certain you are allowed to make notes once you are in the testing site; not all locations will permit it. Once you get your test, on a small piece of paper write down everything you are afraid you will forget. It will take a minute or two but by dumping your worries onto the page you have effectively eliminated a certain amount of anxiety and driven off the panic you feel.

Get comfortable in your chair

Here is a clever technique that releases physical stress and helps you get comfortable, even relaxed in your body. You will tense and hold each of your muscles for just a few seconds. The trick is, you must tense them hard for the technique to work. You might want to practice this technique a few times at home; you do not want an unfamiliar technique to add to your stress just before a test, after all! Once you are at the test site, this exercise can always be done in the rest room or another quiet location.

Start with the muscles in your face then work down your body. Tense, squeeze and hold the muscles for a moment or two. Notice the feel of every muscle as you go down your body. Scowl to tense your forehead, pull in your chin to tense your neck. Squeeze your shoulders down to tense your back. Pull in your stomach all the way back to your ribs, make your lower back tight then stretch your fingers. Tense your leg muscles and calves then stretch your feet and your toes. You should be as stiff as a board throughout your entire body.

Now relax your muscles in reverse starting with your toes. Notice how all the muscles feel as you relax them one by one. Once you have released a muscle or set of muscles, allow them to remain relaxed as you proceed up your body. Focus on how you are feeling as all the tension leaves. Start breathing deeply when you get to your chest muscles. By the time you have found your chair, you will be so relaxed it will feel like bliss!

Fight distraction

A lucky few are able to focus deeply when taking an important examination, but most people are easily distracted, probably because they would rather be any place else! There are several things you can do to protect yourself from distraction.

Stay away from windows.

If you sit near a window you are adding an unnecessary distraction.

Choose a seat away from the aisle so you do not become distracted by people who leave early. People who leave the exam room early are often the ones who fail. Do not compare your time to theirs.

Of course, you love your friends; that's why they are your friends! In the test room, however, they should become complete strangers inside your mind. Forget they are there. The first step is to distance yourself physically from friends or classmates. That way, you will not be tempted to glance at them to see how they are doing, and there will be no chance of eye contact that could either distract you or even lead to an accusation of cheating. Furthermore, if they are feeling stressed because they did not spend the focused time studying that you did, their anxiety is less likely to permeate your hard-earned calm.

Of course, you will want to choose a seat where there is sufficient light. Nothing is worse than trying to take an important examination under flickering lights or dim bulbs.

Ask the instructor or exam proctor to close the door if there is a lot of noise outside. If the instructor or proctor is unable to do so, block out the noise as best you can. Do not let anything disturb you.

Do not allow yourself to become distracted by being too cold or hot. Regardless of the weather outside, carry a sweater, scarf or jacket if the air conditioning at the test site is set too high, or the heat set too low. By the same token, dress in layers so that you are prepared for a range of temperatures.

Watch Caffeine

Drinking a gallon of coffee or gulping a few energy drinks might seem like a great idea, but it is, in fact, a very bad one. Caffeine, pep pills or other artificial sources of energy are more likely to leave you feeling rushed and ragged. Your brain might be clicking along, all right, but chances are good it is not clicking along on the right track! Furthermore, drinking coffee or energy drinks will mean frequent trips to the rest room. This will cut into the time you should be spending answering questions and is a distraction in itself, since each time you need to leave the room you lose focus. Pep pills will only make it harder to think clearly when solving complicated problems.

At the same time, if anxiety is your problem try to find ways around using tranquilizers during test-taking time. Even medically prescribed anti-anxiety medication can make you less alert and even decrease your motivation. Motivation is what you need to get you through an exam. If your anxiety is so bad that it threatens to interfere with your ability to take an exam, speak to your doctor and ask for documentation. Many testing sites will allow non-distracting test rooms, extended testing time and other accommodations with a doctor's note that explains the situation is made available.

Keep Breathing

It might not make a lot of sense, but when people become anxious, tense, or scared, their breathing becomes shallow and, sometimes stop breathing all together! Pay attention to your emotions, and when you are feeling worried, focus on your breathing. Take a moment to remind yourself to breathe deeply and regularly. Drawing in steady, deep breaths energizes the body. When you continue to breathe deeply you will notice you exhale all the tension.

If you feel you need to, try rehearsing breathing at home. With continued practice of this relaxation technique, you will begin to know the muscles that tense up under pressure. Call these your "signal muscles." These are the ones that will speak to you first, begging you to relax. Take the time to listen to those muscles and do as they ask. With just a little breathing practice, you will get into the habit of checking yourself regularly and when you realize you are tense, relaxation will become second nature.

Avoid Anxiety Before a Test

Manage your time effectively

This is a key to your success! You need blocks of uninterrupted time to study all the pertinent material. Creating and maintaining a schedule will help keep you on track, and will remind family members and friends that you are not available. Under no circumstances should you change your blocks of study time to accommodate someone else, or cancel a study session to do something more fun. Do not interfere with your study time for any reason!

Relax

Use whatever works best for you to relieve stress. Some folks like a good, calming stretch with yoga, others find expressing themselves through journaling to be useful. Some hit the floor for a series of crunches or planks, and still others take a slow stroll around the garden. Integrate a little relaxation time into your schedule, and treat that time, too, as sacred.

Eat healthy

Instead of reaching for the chips and chocolate, fresh fruits and vegetables are not only yummy but offer nutritional benefits that help to relieve stress. Some foods accelerate stress instead of reducing it and should be avoided. Foods that add to higher anxiety include artificial sweeteners, candy and other sugary foods, carbonated sodas, chips, chocolate, eggs, fried foods, junk foods, processed foods, red meat, and other foods containing preservatives or heavy spices. Instead, eat a bowl of berries and some yogurt!

Get plenty of ZZZZZZZs

Do not cram or try to do an all-nighter. If you created a study schedule at the beginning, and if you have stuck with that schedule, have confidence! Staying up too late trying to cram in last-minute bits of information is going to leave you exhausted the next day. Besides, whatever new information you cram in will only displace all the important ideas you've spent weeks learning. Remember: You need to be alert and fully functional the day of the exam

Have confidence in yourself!

Everyone experiences some anxiety when taking a test, but exhibiting a positive attitude banishes anxiety and fills you with the knowledge you really do know what you need to know. This is your opportunity to show how well prepared you are. Go for it!

Be sure to take everything you need

Depending on the exam, you may be allowed to have a pen or pencil, calculator, dictionary or scratch paper with you. Have these gathered together along with your entrance paperwork and identification so that you are sure you have everything that is needed.

Do not chitchat with friends

Let your friends know ahead of time that it is not anything personal, but you are going to ignore them in the test room! Find a seat away from doors and windows, one that has good lighting, and get comfortable. If other students are worried their anxiety could be detrimental to you; of course, you do not have to tell your friends that. If you are afraid they will be offended, tell them you are protecting them from your anxiety!

COMMON TEST-TAKING MISTAKES

Taking a test is not much fun at best. When you take a test and make a stupid mistake that affects your grade negatively, it is natural to be upset, especially when it is something that could have been easily avoided. So what are some of the common mistakes that are made on tests?

Put your name on the test!

How could you possibly forget to put your name on a test?

You would be amazed at how often that happens. Very often, tests without names are thrown out immediately, resulting in a failing grade.

Marking the wrong multiple-choice answer

It is important to work at a steady pace, but that does not mean bolting through the questions. Be sure the answer you are marking is the one you mean to. If the bubble you need to fill in or the answer you need to circle is 'C', do not allow yourself to get distracted and select 'B' instead.

Answering a question twice

Some multiple-choice test questions have two very similar answers. If you are in too much of a hurry, you might select them both. Remember that only one answer is correct, so if you choose more than one, you have automatically failed that question.

Mishandling a difficult question

We recommend skipping difficult questions and returning to them later, but beware! First, be certain that you do return to the question. Circling the entire passage or placing a large question mark beside it will help you spot it when you are reviewing your test. Secondly, if you are not careful to skip the question, you can mess yourself up badly. Imagine that a question is too difficult and you decide to save it for later. You read the next question, which you know the answer to, and you fill in that answer. You continue to the end of the test then return to the difficult question only to discover you didn't actually skip it! Instead, you inserted the answer to the following question in the spot reserved for the harder one, thus throwing off the remainder of your test!

Incorrectly Transferring an answer from scratch paper

This can happen easily if you are trying to hurry! Double check any answer you have figured out on scratch paper, and make sure what you have written on the test itself is an exact match!

Thinking too much

Generally, your first thought is your best thought. If you worry yourself into insecurity, your self-doubts can trick you into choosing an incorrect answer.

CONCLUSION

Congratulations! You have made it this far because you have applied yourself diligently to practicing for the exam and no doubt improved your potential score considerably! Getting into a good school is a huge step in a journey that might be challenging at times but will be many times more rewarding and fulfilling. That is why being prepared is so important.

Study then Practice and then Succeed!

Good Luck!

REGISTER FOR FREE UPDATES AND MORE PRACTICE TEST QUESTIONS

Register your purchase at

https://www.test-preparation.ca/register/ for fast and convenient access to updates, errata, free test tips and more practice test questions.

Learn to increase your score using time-tested secrets for answering multiple choice questions!

This practice book has everything you need to know about answering multiple choice questions on a standardized test!

You will learn 12 strategies for answering multiple choice questions and then practice each strategy with over 45 reading comprehension multiple choice questions, with extensive commentary from exam experts!

Maybe you have read this kind of thing before, and maybe feel you don't need it, and you are not sure if you are going to buy this Book.

Remember though, it only a few percentage points divide the PASS from the FAIL students.

Even if our multiple choice strategies increase your score by a few percentage points, isn't that worth it?

www.multiple-choice.ca

ONLINE RESOURCES

How to Prepare for a Test - The Ultimate Guide

https://www.test-preparation.ca/prepare-test/

Learning Styles - The Complete Guide

https://www.test-preparation.ca/learning-style/

Test Anxiety Secrets!

https://www.test-preparation.ca/test-anxiety/

Time Management on a Test

https://www.test-preparation.ca/time-management/

Flash Cards - The Complete Guide

https://www.test-preparation.ca/flash-cards/

Test Preparation Video Series

https://www.test-preparation.ca/test-video/

How to Memorize - The Complete Guide

https://www.test-preparation.ca/memorize/

Online Library of Student Tips and Strategies

https://www.test-preparation.ca/students-say/